WALK GUIDE

EAST OF IRELAND

Third Edition

Jean Boydell, David Herman & Miriam Joyce McCarthy

GENERAL EDITOR
JOSS LYNAM

GW00689561

Gill & Macmillan

Gill & Macmillan Ltd
Goldenbridge
Dublin 8
with associated companies throughout the world

© Jean Boydell, David Herman and Miriam Joyce McCarthy, 1991, 1996, 1998
Maps drawn by Justin May and the late Nuala Creagh
0 7171 2722 2

Print origination by
Typeform Repro Ltd, Dublin
and Carole Lynch

Printed by
ColourBooks Ltd, Dublin

Based on the Ordnance Survey
by permission of the Government
(Permit No. 5429)

A catalogue record for this book is available
from the British Library.

1   3   5   4   2

CONTENTS

Mountain Safety 1
Protecting the Countryside 2
    The Farmland Code of Conduct 2
Maps and Scales 3
Walking Times 4
Climate and Weather 5

East 7
Introduction 7
    Access and Accommodation 8
    Geology 10
    Flora and Fauna 13
    Key Map East 19
1.   Howth Head 20
2.   Bray Head 22
3.   Three Rock and Fairy Castle 24
4.   Little Sugar Loaf 26
5.   Great Sugar Loaf 26
6.   Seahan and Seefingan 28
7.   Seefingan, Kippure and Coronation Plantation 30
8.   Glencullen 32
9.   The Tonduffs and Maulin from Crone 34
10. Djouce and War Hill 36
11. Fancy, Coffin Stone and Djouce 38
12. Ballinrush Gates to Lough Dan 40
13. Scarr and Knocknacloghoge from Oldbridge 42
14. Easy Circuit of Lough Dan 44
15. Circuit of Glenbride 46
16. Lugnagun, Sorrel and Black Hill 48
17. Mullaghcleevaun and Tonelagee 50
18. Fair Mountain and Lough Firrib 52
19. Three Lakes and Art's Cross 54
20. The Spink and the Derrybawn Ridge 56
21. Glenealo, Turlough Hill and Camaderry 58
22. Carriglinneen and Mullacor 60
23. Glenmalure, the Fraughan Rock Glen and Lugnaquilla 62
24. Ballybraid and Mullacor 64
25. Table Mountain and the Lugduffs 66
26. Carrawaystick and Croaghanmoira 68
27. Circuit of Imaal 70
28. Church Mountain and Lobawn 72

29.	Keadeen	74
30.	Slievemaan	76
31.	Circuit of the Ow Valley	78
32.	Croghan Mountain	80
33.	Blackstairs Mountain	82
34.	Mount Leinster from the South	84
35.	Mount Leinster and Ballycrystal	86

Southeast and Midlands 88
	Introduction	88
	Access and Accommodation	89
	Geology	90
	Flora and Fauna	92
	Antiquities	96
	Key Map Southeast and Midlands	97
36.	Brandon Hill	98
37.	Slievenamon	100
38.	Long Hill and Laghtnafrankee	102
39.	Knockanaffrin Ridge	104
40.	Crotty's Lake and Rock	106
41.	The Circuit of Coumshingaun	108
42.	The Mahon Falls and Coumtay	110
43.	Crohaun	112
44.	Circuit of the Nire Valley	113
45.	Seefin and Farbreaga Horseshoe	116
46.	The Fred Carew Memorial Walk	118
47.	Knockmealdown-Sugarloaf Horseshoe	120
48.	Knockmealdown from the Northern Valleys	122
49.	The Eastern Knockmealdowns	124
50.	The Western Knockmealdowns	126
51.	Knocknafallia from Mount Melleray	128
52.	The East Munster Way: Carrick-on-Suir to Clonmel	130
53.	The East Munster Way: Clonmel to Clogheen	132
54.	Temple Hill-Monabrack Horseshoe	134
55.	Galty Wall and Galtymore	136
56.	Galtymore by the 'Black Road'	138
57.	Galtymore, Galtybeg, O'Loughnan's Castle from Mountain Lodge Youth Hostel	140
58.	Galtymore from the Glencush Boreen	142
59.	Circuit of Lake Muskry	144
60.	Glencush Horseshoe	146
61.	Ballydavid Wood Youth Hostel to Mountain Lodge Youth Hostel	148
62.	Galty Ridge Walk	150

Key Map to Galtee Mountain Walks 153
63. The Ballyhoura Mountains 154
64. Silvermines and Keeper Hill 156
65. Glenletter Circuit 158
66. Glenbarrow Circuit 160
67. The Devil's Bit 163
Bibliography 164
    General 164
    East 164
    South and Midlands 164
Glossary 166

About the Series Editor

Joss Lynam is the doyen of Irish mountaineers. He has
climbed extensively in the Himalayas and the Alps as
well as in Britain and Ireland. He is General Editor of all
three titles in the Irish Walk Guide series and Editor of
Best Irish Walks. He is an officer of the International
Association of Mountaineers, edits *Irish Mountain Log*,
and is deeply involved in developing way-marked trails
in Ireland. He lives in Dublin with his wife Nora,
a keen hill-walker.

MOUNTAIN SAFETY

The Irish hills are still relatively unfrequented. This is a happy situation for hill-walkers unless they get into serious trouble and need help. As this may well have to come from a considerable distance, it is particularly important to take all reasonable precautions.

1. Wear suitable clothing, and regardless of the weather carry extra warm clothes, wind- and water-proof anorak and overtrousers. Except on short, easy walks it is best to wear walking boots.

2. Plan your walk carefully and be sure you can complete it before dark. To estimate walking times see page 4.

3. Check weather forecasts and keep a look out for weather changes. On high ground mist and rain can close in with alarming speed.

4. Remember that the temperature drops 2–3°C for each 300m/1,000ft you climb and if, as is frequently the case, there is a strong wind the temperature drop will be even more marked. It may be a pleasant day at sea level whilst freezing and windy at 800m/2,500ft.

5. Always carry a map and compass, and learn to use them efficiently in good weather so you will have confidence in your ability to use them in bad. A torch, whistle and small first aid kit should also be taken — remember that the mountain distress signal is six blasts per minute and then a pause.

6. Carry a reserve supply of food including chocolate, glucose tablets, etc., and something warm to drink.

7. Leave word at your hotel, guesthouse or hostel where you are going, what your route will be and when you intend to get back. If you are parking a car at the beginning of a walk, you can leave a note on the seat.

8. Streams in flood are dangerous and extreme caution is necessary.

9. If your party does have an accident, telephone 999 and ask for the Mountain Rescue or contact the local Garda Station who will organise the rescue.

10. Never walk solo, except in areas where there are other people around.

11. Remember that most accidents happen on the descent, when you are tired, so take especial care then.

Some of the precautions listed above are obviously designed for the longer, higher walks but do remember that especially in winter, the Irish hills can be dangerous.

PROTECTING THE COUNTRYSIDE

Ireland has recently introduced a new Occupiers' Liability Act — dealing with the liability of farmers or other landowners for accidents which may happen to a walker or other user crossing their land. The act creates a new category of 'Recreational Users' who, when they enter farmland, are responsible for their own safety and for the safety of any children in their care. It is to be hoped that this will make farmers, who have been worried about the possibility of claims following accidents to walkers, more willing to permit walkers to cross their land. The Irish Farmers Association, working with the Mountaineering Council of Ireland and other user bodies, has drawn up the following code to which all walkers and other users should adhere:

The Farmland Code of Conduct

* Respect farmland and the rural environment.
* Do not interfere with livestock, crops, machinery or any other property which does not belong to you.
* Guard against all risks of fire.
* Leave all farm gates as you find them.
* Always keep children under close control and supervision.
* Avoid entering farmland containing livestock. Your presence can cause stress to livestock and even endanger your own safety.
* Do not enter farmland if you have dogs with you, even on a leash, unless with the permission of the occupier.
* Always use gates, stiles or other recognised entry points.
* Take all litter home.
* Do not pollute water supplies.
* Take special care on country roads.
* Avoid making unnecessary noise.
* Protect wildlife, plants and trees.
* Take heed of warning signs — they are there for your protection.
* If following a recognised walking route, keep to the way-marked trail.
* Report any damage caused by your actions to the farmer or landowner immediately.
* Do not block farm entrances when parking.

MAPS AND SCALES

The Republic of Ireland is in the process of a complete re-survey and re-issue of its small-scale maps, changing from imperial to metric units. All the walks in this volume are covered by new 1:50,000 scale maps.

These new maps replace a set of half-inch to one mile maps, which are out of date, and on too small a scale to be useful to the walker. They are still in print, but we do not recommend you to use them. Many of the sketch maps in this guide were drawn a few years ago, and the metric heights on them may differ by a couple of metres from the heights on the new maps.

The new maps are based on air survey, with a variable amount of ground checking. They are excellent on contours and natural features, but are not entirely dependable in the marking of tracks and paths.

The sketch maps in this book will give you a good idea of your route, but they are hardly sufficient as complete guides, especially on the more mountainous walks, and you are strongly advised to use the relevant topographical map.

Since distances on some rural signposts are still in miles, and because most cars in Ireland still have mileometers, we have used both miles and kilometres for approaches by car. For easy reference we have used both imperial and metric measurements for the total length and height gain of each walk.

Ordnance Survey maps:
1:250,000 Holiday Map. Sheets 2, 3 and 4.
These are suitable for general planning.
1:50,000 (1¼ ins to 1 mile) map. Sheets 50, 54, 56, 59, 62, 67,68, 73, 74 and 75.

Other useful maps:
Glendalough 1:25,000 (Wicklow National Park)
Comeragh Mountains 1:25,000 (E. Ryan, Clonanav)
East Munster Way Map Guide (1:50,000). (East West Mapping, Ballyredmond, Clonegal, Co. Wexford)

WALKING TIMES

Walking times have been calculated on the basis of 4km per hour, and 400m ascent per hour. This is roughly equivalent to 2½ miles per hour, and nearly 1,300ft ascent per hour. These are fairly generous, and should allow you the occasional stop to admire the view, look at the map, take photographs, or recover your breath. They do not allow for protracted lunch stops! Extra time has been allowed if the going is difficult, and vice versa.

CLIMATE AND WEATHER

The climate of the east and southeast of Ireland, like that of the whole island, is shaped by two factors, the westerly atmospheric circulation and the proximity of the Atlantic Ocean. These factors interact to give us westerly winds, mild damp weather and a small temperature range throughout the year.

Although the weather is very variable, certain climatic features seem to occur with some regularity. During December and January, there is a well-established low-pressure system over the Atlantic, producing depressions which move rapidly eastwards bringing strong winds and abundant frontal rain. By late January the cold anti-cyclonic weather centred over Europe may be extending westwards into Ireland giving dry, cold spells, eminently suitable for hill-walking. From February to June the cold European anti-cyclones tend to produce the driest period of the year. Towards late June or early July the pressure rises over the ocean and falls over the continent, initiating a westerly, damp airflow over Ireland. Cloud cover, humidity and rainfall increase and thunder becomes more prevalent, especially during the warmer periods of August. Cold northerly air may bring active depressions in late August and September, but these can be interrupted by spells of anti-cyclonic weather. In October and November rain-bearing westerlies predominate, though an incursion of anti-cyclonic conditions can bring blue skies and pleasant walking conditions. The prevailing winds are south-westerly and westerly, but winds from the north and east may occur with anti-cyclonic conditions. The winds are lightest from June to September, and strongest from November to March.

May tends to be the sunniest month with around six hours per day, falling away through June to four and a half hours per day in July.

As noted above, the spring is the driest part of the year, and though the ground underfoot is still very wet from the autumn and winter rains, March, April and May are perhaps the best months for walking.

In general rainfall decreases as one moves east, though this tendency is hardly noticeable in the mountain areas. Snow is uncommon in our maritime climate, rarely persisting for long, even at high level, though in some winters it may lie for several weeks in high north-facing coums and gullies.

Looking more closely at the east, we find the highest average annual rainfall near the highest peaks and along the ridges connecting them. Near Lugnaquilla the average rainfall is about 2,400mm and near Kippure it is about 2,000mm. This compares with 700mm in Dublin City, about 800mm on the plains of Kildare and about 900mm along the Wicklow coast. There is no significant tendency for the western slopes to be wetter than the eastern slopes. In general, rainfall increases with elevation above sea level. However, deep narrow valleys in the mountains (e.g. Glenmalure) experience nearly as much rain as the mountains surrounding them. Average rainfall varies from month to month. In the Wicklow Mountains, December and January are the wettest months and April and June the driest. An idea of this annual variation is given by the monthly averages (in mm) for the Wicklow Gap over the period 1941–70.

Jan.	Feb.	Mar.	Apr.	May	June	July	Aug.	Sept.	Oct.	Nov.	Dec.
219	150	117	134	108	108	120	151	176	181	195	243

However, don't let this put you off; armed with waterproof clothing even a showery day can be very pleasant between downpours. Remember the saying 'rain before seven, sun before eleven', which is very true of the mountains in this area.

Looking specifically at the southeastern counties, we find that the mountains receive an average 1,800 to 2,500mm (72 to 100 inches) of rain per annum, mainly from September through to January. The lower hills, particularly those of north Tipperary and Laois/Offaly receive from 1,200 to 2,000mm (48 to 80 inches) annually, whilst the lowland area tends to attract half that recorded in the mountains.

To fully appreciate the way that the high ground attracts the rain one has only to stand in bright sunshine on the plains of the area and see how often the mountains are wreathed in clouds. To further stress the necessity for guarding against the weather in these hills, it should be noted that there are on average 175 to 200 'wet' days annually, these being days on which at least 1mm of rain falls. Some consolation may be gained, however, from the fact that there are less than 90 days per annum without sunshine which suggests that many of the wet days also have their brighter periods.

INTRODUCTION

My first memories of the Wicklow Mountains date from when I was about six. At that impressionable age I remember striding proudly and confidently down to Lough Dan — and being dragged tired and cranky all the way back. Nevertheless, in spite of (because of?) such early impressions it is 'only' in the last 30 years — thus leaving a yawning gap of 20 — that I have really got to know the Wicklow Mountains and it is as recently as the last ten that I have set foot in the Blackstairs.

In those 30 years the popularity of hill-walking has increased in quantum leaps. Where once one could wander without meeting a soul, now, even on weekdays, it is unusual not to meet someone. As for Sundays . . . well, up to 50 or even 60 people might be out in one group and several large groups might be encountered in the course of a day's walking. Shades of Dublin's O'Connell Street! It would be mean-minded not to welcome this great increase in numbers even if it leads to paths being eroded and the remoteness of the hills being lost. After all, apart from the obvious fact that hill-walking is a healthy and participative (and mercifully, non-sponsored) recreation, the people who walk the mountains are the people who enjoy and appreciate them. They are the people who will protect the mountains and our environment generally and who will ultimately make it clear to our political masters that, yes, we do care or put more crudely, that there are votes 'in them thar hills'.

Never was this message of conservation in greater need of being proclaimed from the hill-tops. Not to put a tooth in it: *in general* we as a nation do not care much about our environment. As the inimitable travel writer, Dervla Murphy, once wrote (I paraphrase, I hope not too exaggeratedly): how can people who are surrounded by such natural beauty as we are be content to live in the midst of squalor? The litter on our streets, the sore thumbs of 'haciendas' rawly and incongruously perched on our hill-tops, and the rubbish dumped on our country roads are all manifestations of the same malaise. Too many of us do not care.

Yet all is not gloom. A most hopeful sign is the recent establishment of a National Park in the Wicklow Mountains — above all areas in the Republic, the most threatened by 'development' and deterioration. This is a real indication that we are prepared to protect a fragile and precious heritage. As someone who has pleaded for this for some years I welcome it most warmly. If this area is given the same high degree of protection as the other National Parks in Ireland — and I am sure it will be — we can look forward to the conservation, indeed the enhancement, of the area's beauty and of its amenity and scientific value.

There is one other consequence of the increased numbers walking the hills that I must regretfully mention. That is the pressure that great numbers of hill-walkers put on farmers. We must not be surprised if farmers, especially those close to Dublin, consider themselves under siege. Litter is left strewn around for livestock to eat, fence wire is stood upon, stone walls knocked down, sheep harassed and killed by stray dogs. Of course the average hill-walker though not entirely blameless is not responsible for all this, but someone is, and it is asking a lot of farmers to differentiate between responsible hill-walkers and uncouth yobbos. We are all likely to be tarred with the one brush: trespassers and destructive trespassers at that.

It would help greatly to defuse tension if statutory rights of way were to be established from motorable roads through farmland to open country above, but given the slow pace of legislative change here and the probable opposition — shortsighted opposition I would suggest — of landowners, I cannot see this development occurring in the near future. In the meantime please take great care in or near enclosed fields. Study the section on Protecting the Countryside and the Farmland Code of Conduct given earlier. And if you are informed that you are trespassing, go politely and without further ceremony.

Having said all this it is necessary to add an important and I hope reassuring rider. Though difficulties are understandably worst near Dublin, away from the city relations between farmers and hill-walkers are much more amicable. Country people are almost invariably friendly and would appreciate a greeting and a few words of chat. Don't pass by in surly silence.

It is usual in the introduction to guidebooks to suggest modestly that the routes given are only a selection and that the user of the guide should use the book as a base for further exploration. And it's true of this guide. One of the great attractions of Irish mountains — and I say this in particular to overseas visitors — is that the terrain generally encourages a wide wandering. Once you reach the uplands you can wander more or less where you will. It's all waiting for *you* to explore!

Lastly I would like to thank my wife Mairin Geraty for walking many of the routes with me over the years and for her forthright comments on sloppiness in my prose (remaining sloppiness is of course my responsibility). I would also like to thank Joss Lynam, who asked me to co-author this book and who as ever gave, with his usual good humour, his time unstintingly and his expert advice ungrudgingly.

ACCESS AND ACCOMMODATION
ACCESS BY CAR: We will, we hope, be excused if we describe access to the Wicklow Mountains, the area which is likely to be most difficult to access, almost entirely from the viewpoint of the Dublin-based walker. If you don't

start from the capital there are few problems of access that the appropriate maps won't solve.

For the eastern side take the N11/M11 to Kilmacanoge, turning right here onto the R755 for the Lough Tay/Lough Dan area, Glendalough and Glenmalure. The alternative route along the eastern flank is to take the R117 to Enniskerry, a scenic but narrow road which takes you through the spectacular defile of the Scalp.

The Military Road (designated R115) is a high-level scenic route which runs the entire length of the Wicklow Mountains. For a quick exercise-free introduction to these mountains the Military Road to Glenmalure is unbeatable. Incidentally, it has the highest point of tarmac in Ireland (excluding cul-de-sacs) at 525m just north of Sally Gap.

For the western side take the N81 to or through Blessington. This road has good views of Pollaphuca Reservoir and the hills on the west of the Wicklow Mountains.

There are two *high-level east–west roads*. The more northerly is the Sally Gap road (R759) which runs from the R755 in the east past the dramatically beautiful Lough Tay area and crosses the Military Road at Sally Gap. From here it descends gradually to the N81 near Kilbride. The more southerly is the Wicklow Gap Road (R756) which runs from Glendalough, reaches its highest point, 478m, close to Tonelagee and then descends parallel to the Kings River passing through Hollywood to reach the N81.

A general point. It is regrettable to have to say that you should leave no valuables visible, better you should leave no valuables at all, in cars parked anywhere in the Wicklow Mountains. In recent years there have been numerous break-ins to cars even in remote car parks.

TRAIN AND BUS SERVICES: DART services to Bray are frequent and inexpensive but the only other possibly useful train service is that to Rathdrum. Dublin Bus provides a good service to many places in or near the Wicklow (and Dublin) Mountains. Those to Ballyknockan (65 bus route), Barnacullia (44B), Blessington (65), Bohernabreena (49A), Enniskerry (44), Glencullen (44B), Rockbrook (47A) and Shop River west of Enniskerry (185) are particularly useful but check times as some services are very infrequent.

There is also a privately operated bus service run by the St Kevin's Bus Company. The route is from St Stephen's Green West, Dublin to Glendalough taking in Kilmacanoge, Roundwood and Laragh. Details from the company at Roundwood, Co. Wicklow (Tel. 01-281 8119).

One last point for those using public transport. In general, if you are based in Dublin, it will be better for your peace of mind to walk northwards rather than south. This is because the bus service is more frequent nearer the city, that is, at the north of the range. It is easy enough to catch that solitary long-distance bus in the morning when you can judge your time accurately; then you can avail of the frequent local bus service in the evening when you can't.

Irish Bus (Bus Eireann) provincial bus services go to Blessington, Annalecky Cross (for Donard) and Baltinglass on the west of the Wicklow Mountains, Kilmacanoge and Rathdrum on the east; and Bagenalstown (Muine Bheag), Bunclody, Kiltealy and Graiguenamanagh for the Blackstairs. Check times carefully beforehand as none of these services is frequent.

ACCOMMODATION: If you prefer somewhere a little more peaceful than Dublin, there is plenty of accommodation in Blessington in the west, and more limited accommodation in many towns and villages in other mountain areas in Wicklow. Enniscorthy, Borris, Bunclody, Bagenalstown (Muine Bheag) and Graiguenamanagh are good bases from which to explore the Blackstairs. There are, of course, isolated houses in the countryside offering accommodation. Details of most hotel, guesthouse and farmhouse accommodation are given in brochures issued by Bord Failte (Irish Tourist Board).

So to the more modest. There are seven youth hostels in or near the mountains. Serving the northwest is Baltyboys (986 110), delightfully located on a peninsula on Pollaphuca Reservoir but a little far from the hills. Further east are Knockree (192 150) and Glencree (140 179), both in Glencree. Glendalough is suitable for exploring the central area of Wicklow. Further south are Ballinclea (961 952) in the Glen of Imaal and Glenmalure (057 947), which is a small, remote hostel and not always open. Lastly Aghavannagh (060 874) is at the southern end of the Military Road. To avail of hostel accommodation you have to be a member of a national youth hostel organisation. It is also advisable to book in advance. Further details available from An Oige, 61 Mountjoy Street, Dublin 7 (Tel. 01-830 4555, Fax 01-830 5808).

There is also a number of 'independent hostels', privately owned, of similar comfort level to An Oige hostels. There are no membership restrictions — anyone can use them. They belong to two organisations. For details contact:

Irish Holiday Hostels Association (IHHA), 57 Lower Gardiner Street, Dublin 1 (Tel. 01-836 4700, Fax 01-836 4710) — these are all Bord Failte approved.

Independent Hostels Organisation (IHO), Dooey Hostel, Glencolumbkille, Co. Donegal (Tel. 073-30130, Fax 073-30339).

Lastly, spartan types might consider camping. The only camping site near the mountains is at Roundwood. Nevertheless it is possible to camp almost anywhere but please ask the landowner's permission first. This injunction does not apply if you intend camping on bleak mountain tops!

GEOLOGY

The structure of the mountains should not be dismissed as being of merely academic interest to the walker. The type of rock in a region largely determines the terrain, is the basic material for the soil which develops above it, and so influences the vegetation and ultimately the animal life. Of course, vegetation and animal life are influenced by geology to only a limited degree, climate being the major factor. A knowledge of the geology of an area, however, provides a good indication of its other fundamental characteristics.

Standing on Bray Head, or Howth Head further north, the observer will be struck by the contrast between the hills along the eastern seaboard and those further west forming the crest of the range. The hills on the east are small but craggy and precipitous knobs and those to the west higher, but with gentle, softly-rounded domes.

The explanation for this and similar contrasts lies in the nature and history of the rock types present in the mountain area. The most ancient rocks of the range belong to the Cambrian period (360 million years ago) and are exposed in an irregular, roughly triangular, area of northeast County Wicklow and southeast County Dublin. The peaks in this area are formed of highly resistant green and purple quartzites and have a characteristic bumpiness. In the lower lands lie beds of slate, quartz and sandstone. All these ancient rocks have been so twisted and contorted, broken and eroded through a period long even in geological terms, that their complete history has never been deciphered and undoubtedly never will be. In spite of the local assumption that attributes these rocks to volcanic action — and looking at the sharp cone of Great Sugar Loaf this does not seem unreasonable — all these rocks were laid in fact at the bottom of a shallow sea.

In later times, during the Ordovician period, another deeper sea stretched across what is now Ireland, depositing beds of sedimentary rocks — shales, slates and sandstones — on its floor. When these rocks were eventually exposed to the air — due to the lifting of the ocean floor or the sinking of the sea — a subdued plain lay where the mountains of the east of Ireland now rise.

This terrain, with the central mountain core as yet unborn, existed for about 200 million years. Then molten lava, responding to some immense subterranean disturbance, welled up in a great northeast to southwest belt from below the older Ordovician rocks, forcing them into an enormous arch above it and completely altering the zone of Ordovician rock with which it came into contact. Eventually the lava cooled and solidified into the familiar granite of today — by far the largest granite area in this island. The Ordovician arch has almost completely weathered away, exposing the granite underneath in turn to the relentless assault of the elements.

Granite, in spite of its proverbial hardness, is particularly susceptible to chemical weathering: hence the rounded domes of the central granite massif. The zone of former Ordovician rock which came into contact with the molten lava was metamorphosed into a flinty, flaky rock called mica-schist. The rock gives rise to a line of sharp hills and ridges along the granite border. These are more prominent in the east than the west, where the granite plunges more steeply below the Ordovician strata.

The mica-schist contact zone contains ores of lead, copper and iron, which were mined in the eighteenth and nineteenth centuries. The evidence of these workings — slag heaps, smelting houses, workers' dwellings, even rusting, antiquated machinery — litters parts of the valleys of Glenmalure, Glendalough and Glendasan in an unlovely tangle. Fortunately for us, the workings were never on a very large scale and the scars are not very extensive.

The events so far described occurred hundreds of millions of years ago but the first Ice Age (there were at least two in Ireland) began only a million years ago and the last retreated north a mere 10,000 years ago. Since the latter was predominant in determining the present appearance of the mountains of the east, let us look at it now.

At its greatest extent a vast ice sheet, similar to the polar icecaps of today, covered most of the Irish lowlands. Above it the bulk of the mountains protruded like icebergs above a polar sea, but they did not escape the intense cold. At the onset of this Ice Age snow accumulated year after year, firstly on the higher, more sheltered eastern slopes of the hills and secondly, in similarly sheltered nooks and crannies everywhere in the mountains. After many years two great ice fields formed — one from Glenmacnass to the wild country northeast of Sally Gap, the other from Lugnaquilla to the Wicklow Gap. At the same time the ice and snow in the sheltered nooks were carving out the corries of today. These are huge natural amphitheatres, great 'armchairs' complete with 'back', 'arm-rests', and 'seat' — the seat usually occupied by a lake. They are best displayed at both Lough Brays, Powerscourt Deerpark, and the two Prisons of Lugnaquilla. Eventually, from ice field and corrie, the great mass of ice began to move off downhill as mountain glaciers, rivers of ice and snow carrying rocks, boulders and other debris.

It is necessary at this point to compare an unglaciated river valley with a glaciated one. A stream in its upper reaches wends its way between mountain spurs, carving out a channel shaped in cross section like a shallow V. Now suppose a glacier invades such a valley. Because the glacier is so rigid and inflexible it gouges out a path straight down the valley, deepening it from a V into a U and shearing off the mountain spurs. When the glacier finally disappears a straight flat-bottomed valley with precipitous sides has been carved out.

Glenmalure illustrates some typical features of a glacial valley. Here the top of the U-valley is at about 330m, indicated by a sudden change of slope and an irregular line of assorted boulders ('erratics') deposited from the top of the glacier. Above 330m is the remnant of the V-valley; below, cliffs or very steep ground slope down to the flat valley floor of the Avonbeg River. Because the glacier has lowered this valley floor, the valleys of streams tributary to the Avonbeg, which have not been glaciated, are now high above it. These tributary valleys are called 'hanging valleys' and their streams plunge into Glenmalure as waterfalls. The valley of the Carrawaystick Brook is a typical hanging valley.

The moraine is another common glacial phenomenon occurring in Glenmalure. As already mentioned, a glacier transports all sorts of rubble as it grinds forward — boulders, rocks, sand and gravel. But whenever it halts, all the rubble is carried forward to the tongue and dumped there in a long, irregular line spanning the valley. The barracks at Drumgoff (Glenmalure) stand on a moraine, as does the Round Tower at Glendalough. The sandpits around Blessington and the hummocky country near Annamoe are also moraines, but were deposited under somewhat different conditions to those described.

As the climate ameliorated towards the end of the last Ice Age a dramatic physical feature was added to the landscape. This is the glacial spillway, best seen at the Scalp, the Glen of the Downs and the Hollywood Glen, but also elsewhere along the eastern and western flanks of the hills. It originated when, with the improving climate, vast quantities of snow and ice melted and huge lakes formed which were hemmed in between the ice sheets on the plains and the mountain ridges of the hills. Eventually, the rising waters spilled over at the lowest point in the surrounding hills, cutting enormous gashes through them. Their characteristic shape means that they can be easily identified from the contour lines on the map.

Although all areas of the east, as indeed nearly all areas of Ireland, show the effects of glaciation, these effects are more prominent on the east of the range. For example, one of the most pleasant features of the mountain area is the contrast between the deep, narrow, straight glens of the east, which are highly glaciated, and the lightly glaciated, shallow open basins of the west which carry the upper reaches of the Slaney, the Liffey and their tributaries. It is to the Ice Age that we owe these and other contrasts, which have added so much to the beauty of the hills.

FLORA AND FAUNA

I now move on to the plant, bird and animal life of the mountains. I have tried to keep the summary brief but at the same time to give the casual reader an idea of what constitutes the flora and fauna of the area. I have also tried to mention items which he or she may come across while walking in these mountains.

FLORA: The dominant character of the mountains of the east is formed by the forest plantations. Great zones of colour sweep the hillside contours giving suitable contrast to otherwise bleak mountain scenery. The main coniferous components of the area are the larch, which is soft green in spring and summer but pale and yellow in autumn, mingled with the dark greens of Sitka spruce and Corsican pine, and with belts of blue-green Scots pine, which has a reddish, gaunt and flat-topped appearance in maturity. Occasional patches of silver fir, boasting large resin-coated cones, are a feature of Djouce Woods.

Birch, rowan, ash, alder, hawthorn and holly are fairly common on the mountainside. They are of great importance as sources of food and shelter for both bird and insect life. Occasionally stands of aspen are encountered, in places such as the approach to Lugnaquilla above the Fraughan Rock Glen in Glenmalure. But the tree of prime importance in Wicklow is the oak (*Quercus robur*). It is limited to areas such as the Glen of the Downs and Glendalough and a few specimens are found in the Devil's Glen, Glencree and on the approaches to Lough Dan and Lough Tay. It is within an oak forest that one quickly learns to appreciate the forest environment. Oak galls with their larva inside, moss and lichen growth on stems (indicators of low air pollution), leaf galls and consequently heavy leaf litter which makes underfoot conditions pleasant, all add together to make a walk in this type of environment a most memorable experience. Plants within the oak domain vary from climbers, such as honeysuckle, to bulbs, such as the bluebell. On the fringe, primroses sometimes occur with a sprinkling of the invading rhododendron. In a native environment the introduction of aliens such as the rhododendron can lead to complete imbalance with natural regenerating tree and shrub species being suppressed.

The mountain terrain is a very bleak and difficult site for the development of a plant community. Constant wind, heavy rainfall, poor soil and an ever-increasing sheep population all limit plant life. Many areas of the mountains are covered by ling (*Calluna*) heather (*Erica*), giving a characteristic purple tinge to the hills during August and September. As this plant gets older, vast frameworks of woody stems are produced. Ultimately controlled burning is carried out, which leads to fresh regrowth the following spring, and provides a welcome bite for the sheep. However, over-zealous grazing or burning can lead to invasion by bracken. With its brittle stem and vast hoards of midges and flies most walkers are only too familiar with this plant. An annual, it dies back each winter, often making winter walking a more pleasant pastime.

The poor peatland soils on top of gentle bedrock are lacking in nitrogen, an essential element in plant development. Plants adapt in different ways to cope with this problem. Some have the ability to fix atmospheric nitrogen, such as alder, broom and gorse. Others have become more ingenious, namely the sundew. Its tiny leaves are modified to form a trap for unsuspecting insects and are as deadly as a spider's web. A sticky exudation covers each leaf. Insects that are attracted alight on the leaves, which move inwards to envelop the prey and digest the body fluids by enzymes. Protein is broken down into amino acid and nitrogen. The valley area surrounding the Raven's Glen is a very good one in which to find examples, but you need to be observant. The best time is about mid July.

While the mountain flora is distinctly poor, due to height and exposure, certain unusual plants are to be found on Lugnaquilla, including clubmoss. Its scaly, green, silky stems are a sure indicator that you are high up on the mountain. St Patrick's Cabbage (*Saxifraga umbrosa*), a rare Pyrenean plant, has also been found in this location. At lower altitudes, especially in the Sally Gap and on the approach to Kippure, purple loosestrife, with its bright purple plumes, can be seen in combination with bog cotton. The Upper Lake at Glendalough is also an area of botanical interest: white waterlilies grow in the calm water near the shoreline and a belt of Scots pine flanks the shore. Here witches brooms occur. These are caused by an insect feeding on the growing shoots of pine trees. The cells react by forming a tumour-like growth, which has a twisted, contorted habit and grows very slowly.

FAUNA: The fauna of the mountains of the east is quite varied despite the increasing disturbance caused by the motorised public, who seem to drive their vehicles further from the county roads each year. This movement of people and their associated picnic waste has resulted in an increase in the populations of the raven (*Corvus corax*) and the hooded crow (*Corvus corone cornix*) due to the increased food supply. But the advantages of human disturbance are outweighed by the disadvantages. Each year more habitat is being destroyed and so we are losing different species from particular areas year by year.

In the lower areas and in the vicinity of agricultural land one may find the fieldfare (*Turdus pilaris*) and mistle thrush (*Turdus viscivorus*) among the birds normally associated with suburban gardens. In addition, a common sight is that of a kestrel (*Falco tinnunculus*) hovering for long periods before suddenly swooping on some prey such as a fieldmouse (*Sylvaemus sylvaticus*). Starlings (*Sturnus vulgaris*), while in small groups during the summer months, can, with the advent of winter and swelled in numbers by immigrants, be seen in huge flocks numbering several thousand moving en masse from field to field. The jackdaw (*Corvus monedula*) and rook (*Corvus frugilegus*) behave in a similar manner. Starling roosts are found in some coniferous forests, where the stench of droppings can be sufficient to nauseate even the hardiest of walkers. The robin (*Erithacus rubecula*) although normally associated with suburban back gardens, is a common sight in the diverse habitat of our woodlands. In common with the robin, the great tit (*Parus major*), coal tit (*Parus ater*), blue tit (*Parus caeruleus*) and the long tailed tit (*Aegilthalos caudatus*) share the habitat, generally moving about in small groups and drawing attention to themselves by constant twittering. The pheasant (*Phasianus colchicus*) will most likely betray its presence by a sudden vertical take-off accompanied by loud whirring wing noises. Another bird of the woodlands, with interesting feeding habits, is the tree creeper (*Certhia familiaris*), which climbs up trees spirally in short bursts with its stiff tail pressed against the bark, while using its thin curved bill to search for insects in bark crevices.

Among gorse and heather one may find the linnet (*Acanthis cannabina*), redpoll (*Acanthis flammea*) and whinchat (*Saxicola rubetra*). In summer the meadow pipit (*Anthus pratensis*) and the skylark (*Alauda arvensis*), with its musical outpourings at great height, move to the hills from lower ground. The twite (*Acanthis flavirostris*) is found in this region also, but can be confused with the linnet.

Associated with streams and ponds are the grey wagtail (*Motacilla cinerea*), dipper (*Cinclus cinclus*) and perhaps, in quieter waters, the kingfisher (*Alcedo atthis*) and grey heron (*Ardea cinerea*), the latter standing stock still while preying upon frogs and smaller varieties of fish.

Higher up on the heather moors the most common bird in former times was the red grouse (*Lagopus lagopus scoticus*) but, with the decline in proper grouse moor management, numbers have dropped to seriously low levels. Also in this habitat one can expect to observe the hen harrier (*Circus cyaneus*), one-time predator of the red grouse, hooded crow and raven. The rarest bird of prey in the region is the peregrine falcon (*Falco peregrinus*), which is making a slow comeback to the wilder areas, but at the moment its haunts are closely-guarded secrets.

It is probable that the red fox (*Vulpes vulpes*) is the most talked about animal in rural areas. It has been the scourge of both sheep farmers and gamekeepers alike. However the mink (*Mustela vison*) has now achieved some notoriety in this field and has the reputation of a fierce and wanton killer. It fits into an ecological niche between that of the otter (*Lutra lutra*) and the stoat (*Mustela erminea*). The mink has been largely responsible for the decimation of both the coot (*Fulica atra*) and moorhen (*Gallinula chloropus*) populations of streams and ponds in the eastern half of the country. All the same, it does useful work in keeping the rat (*Rattus norvegicus*) population down to a manageable level. The rabbit (*Oryctolagus cuniculus*) has long been a menace to tillage farmers because of its voracious appetite and reproductive capacity. Nowadays its numbers are much reduced owing to the inroads of myxomatosis.

The state forests, boring as they may look from the outside, and from the inside to some eyes as well, do provide a very diverse habitat for many animals and birds. In the forests where Scots pine and larch are found in sizeable quantity one is sure to observe the red squirrel (*Scuirus vulgaris*) on the ground or streaking up the trunk of a tree. The grey squirrel (*Neoscuirus carolinensis*) is also found, but at present is confined to the northern part of the region.

It is possible to observe the woodmouse (*Sylvaemus sylvaticus*) in most types of woodland. Despite being associated with back gardens, the

16

hedgehog (*Erinaceus europaeus*) is also present and can be seen, mainly at dusk, searching for food in the form of earthworms (*Lumbricus spp*) and the young of the woodmouse and other small rodents. The badger (*Meles meles*) is a common resident of both coniferous and deciduous woodland, making elaborate setts wherever the soil is dry and least compacted.

On open moorland one is likely to find the blue hare (*Lepus timidus*) and on, or adjacent to, grassland the larger brown hare (*Lepus capensis*). It is in this particular vegetation zone that the largest of our wild mammals, the deer (*Cervus spp*), is located. In order to eliminate confusion as regards the deer in County Wicklow it should be noted that all the deer in the upland zone are hybrids of the red deer (*Cervus elaphus*) and the Japanese sika deer (*Cervus nippon*). Some, especially those in the Turlough Hill area, show characteristics of the Japanese sika deer and are termed 'sika-like'. A small number of fallow deer (*Dama dama*) can be found in the Ashford–Rathdrum area. The only other animal population of note found wild in this region is the feral goat (*Capra spp*) which arose from the domestic goat either by escaping or by deliberate releasing of unwanted animals. There are several herds, the one at Glendalough being the best known.

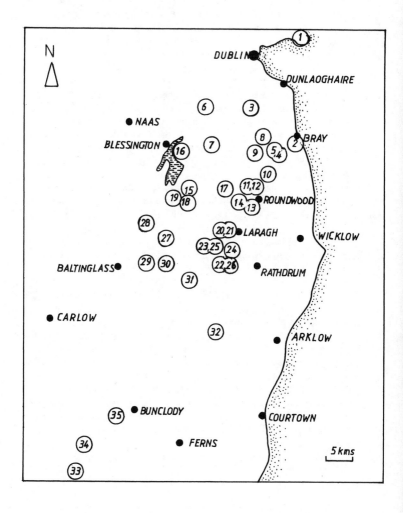

N

DUBLIN

DUNLAOGHAIRE

⑥ ③

● NAAS

BLESSINGTON ● ⑯ ⑦

⑧
⑨ ⑤,④ ② BRAY

⑩
⑰ ⑪,⑫
⑮ ⑭ ● ROUNDWOOD
⑲ ⑬
⑱

⑱ WICKLOW

⑳,㉑ ● LARAGH
㉘
㉗
㉓,㉕ ㉔
㉒,㉖
㉙ ㉚ ● RATHDRUM
BALTINGLASS ●
㉛

● CARLOW

㉜

● ARKLOW

● COURTOWN

㉟ ● BUNCLODY

5 kms

㉞ ● FERNS

㉝

1. HOWTH HEAD

The tiny, rocky hills of Howth Head and its nearby sea cliffs and secluded coves are a favourite area for Dubliners, and no wonder. Here, within a few miles of the city centre, is an area, almost an island, with an atmosphere and terrain quite different to the city's bustling streetscapes. Nevertheless it is partly a built-up area and this precludes any sense of wild remoteness. Better accept it for what it is, a type of suburban wilderness.

Howth is well served by DART and the 31 and 31A bus routes. If travelling by car, park near the DART station.

From the harbour, walk east up Balscadden Road heading for the Cliff Walk. Along the first stretch the cliffs are high and forbidding: an excellent area for sea birds nesting in 'high-rise flats', with the occasional patrol sweeping out over the sea or towards Ireland's Eye. Crossing the road to the Baily Lighthouse on a promontory down on the left, the route takes a path left of the garden of the last house, forking right after a few metres to turn west as imperceptibly as it has already swung from east to south. More noticeably, as the path follows the edge, the rocky cliffs yield seawards to grassy slopes backing tiny, rock-strewn inlets and bony, upward-reaching fingers of ancient rock.

Further along watch out for a wall of seashell, rock and concrete which will be your guiding companion on the right. It turns inland at Red Rock and here you must follow a steep path uphill to tarmac at Carrickbrack Road. Turn left here, walk 250m or so to a path on the right and climb from here to the top of a nearby rocky knoll, Shielmartin. Considering its height, 163m, the views up and down the coast are excellent and the possibility of a sight of the distant, rolling Mournes lends a touch of added interest.

Descend to the cottage tucked in under Shielmartin (in mist or fog continue straight over the top in a northerly direction to a path to the cottage), cross the golf course following a line of white rocks and enter a narrow, heavily-wooded valley between two rocky ridges. At its far end pass by a second golf course on the left, leave the trees and keep straight on a track marked by white stones to playing fields. With the playing fields on the right descend to tarmac at Balkill Road. From here it is but a short downhill stroll to base through some of the more attractive parts of Howth.

Distance: 11.3km/7miles. Ascent: 250m/830ft. Walking time: 3¾ hours.

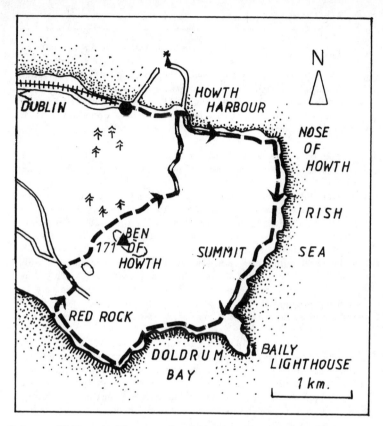

Reference OS Maps: Dublin street plan (1:20,000) or Sheet 50 (1:50,000).

2. BRAY HEAD

It is probably not fully appreciated that height is not a prerequisite for an excellent mountain viewpoint. A low but well-placed vantage point can offer better views than a high summit hemmed in by dull shoulders. Bray Head is an example: a varied and scenic panorama of indented coast, nearby shapely rocky hills and further away rolling domes of the whole northeast of the range, all from a mere 200m high. If you want to spend a half-day you could do a lot worse than sample the scenic and varied walking on lowly Bray Head.

Bray is well served by DART and buses. Travellers by car can drive along the Strand Road (seafront) and park at the southern end in the car park.

From the start of the Cliff Walk climb by any convenient path to the Cross on the hummock which dominates the northern top. This is a rather unkempt and eroded stretch but do not be discouraged: better terrain awaits. At the Cross walk to a track running close to the next rocky hummock. And here I can reveal the great navigational simplicity of this walk: *all* turns from here on are left! So turn left onto the track and walk along a tiny plateau towards the South Top — an upland world of tiny rocky 'haystacks', rough gorse and bracken, the swelling ocean on one side, the small but impressive Sugar Loafs on the other. You might even be lucky enough to see the herd of feral goats whose stamping ground this is. All in all, quite a contrast to busy Bray so close at hand.

The South Top is out of bounds, so you must walk west down the track to a bypassed stretch of road, turn left here and turn left again onto the Bray–Greystones road. Keep on the main road through the hamlet of Windgates, turning left on its far side onto a minor road. Walk to the end of this road. Going left in front of a building (under construction at time of writing), pass through a gate and take the path beyond it, which ends at a stile on the Cliff Walk. Turn left here.

The 2.5km back to Bray are dominated by the wrinkled waters of the ocean stretching away seemingly to infinity: its littoral of ancient rock; the myriads of kittiwakes, gulls, guillemots and shags which depend on it; its erosive power as evidenced by the abandoned railway tunnels. Man, perhaps mercifully, is not yet quite the measure of all things!

Distance: 8km/5miles. Ascent: 240m/800ft. Walking time: 2½ hours.

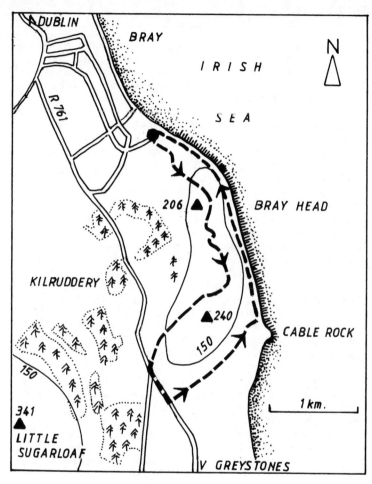

Reference OS Map: Sheet 56 (1:50,000).

3. THREE ROCK AND FAIRY CASTLE

Over the southeast suburbs of Dublin a low plateau modestly rises. Its highest points are Fairy Castle and the granite, tor-topped Three Rock and Two Rock. Given the close proximity of the entire plateau to the city the wonder is that anything worth walking remains. Yet there are some quite pleasant areas left, still preserving a sense of remoteness though so near the metropolis.

You can reach Barnacullia village (181 242) by car, about 1.5km/1mile south of Lamb Doyles pub on Woodside Road. The 44B bus serves Barnacullia but is infrequent. The more frequent 44 bus goes as far as Sandyford. The 44B might be used in one direction though is unlikely to be frequent enough to be used in both.

Walk back towards Dublin from the Blue Light pub, taking the first track on the left (west). Wind left around the first bend to the quarry entrance and go right onto a track. Climb with the track for about five minutes and, before it starts to descend, take either of two paths left. Walk steadily uphill to forest through a gorse and heather area which allows widening views over the city and sea. Follow the edge of the forest to the top of Three Rock, a veritable pincushion of masts bristling just over the horizon. From Three Rock walk southwest to Fairy Castle, 536m, the highest point in the area. On this short stretch there is a plethora of paths and tracks to guide — or confuse — so a compass bearing may be prudent.

From Fairy Castle head southeast for Two Rock, indicated by a heap of stones nearby on the horizon. This heap is emphatically *not* one of the Rocks of Two Rock; these noble granite tors lie disdainfully a little further on, across a forest fence.

We now enter the terrain of forest tracks. Stay outside the fence and follow it south, then southeast downhill. At the second track into the forest, where the ground levels off, cross a stile onto a path through the trees to quickly join the end of a forest track.

Continue on this forest track to a bar, turning right just before it and right at the next junction. At the T-junction below go right again and follow this track as it turns left where another track comes in from the right. Stay on the track to turn left again (a turning circle on the right over the bank confirms, but don't head for it) and come to an unforested section on the right. Continue straight to where the trees start again, going right and following this path as it winds along the edge of the trees to a forest track. Turning right here, this track leads to a bar, then tarmac. At the road below, going left, a walk of 1.5km will take you back to Barnacullia.

Distance: 8.8km/5.5miles. Ascent: 330m/1,100ft. Walking time: 3 hours.

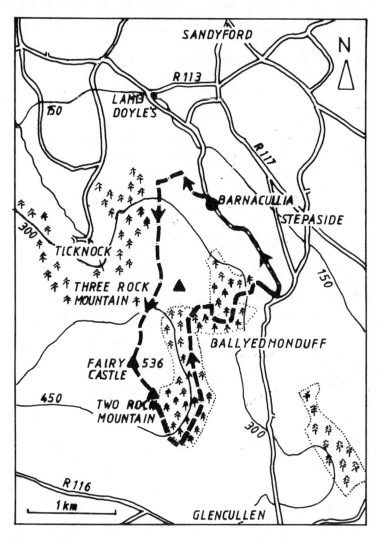

Reference OS Map: Sheet 50 (1:50,000).

4. LITTLE SUGAR LOAF

Little Sugar Loaf, 342m, more an undulating ridge than a peak, runs north to south between Bray Head to the east and Great Sugar Loaf to the west, and gives fine views of both. Like them, it exhibits ancient jagged rock resulting in bold craggy outlines. All in all, it makes a delightful walk.

Go by car or bus to Kilmacanoge village on the N11. Travellers by bus will have to walk from here. Travellers by car (and those who have travelled by bus) should turn east in the village just south of R755 and proceed uphill for 1.3km / 0.8mile to a patch of grass on the left (257 140).

Take the track from the parking place eastward towards the south end of the summit ridge and at this end, where further advance is blocked by a fence and a notice (Private Please Keep Out), turn left to follow a line of trees.

Climb directly to the summit — the first summit anyway. There are three distinct rocky summits, all of which are on the route. Anywhere along the high ground makes a good place for a rest. The views to both east and west — and they can be appreciated from the same spot — are excellent: Wicklow Head, Bray Head, Killiney and Howth thrusting towards the sea; Great Sugar Loaf rising magnificently to the west and overshadowing the rounded domes on the main range behind it.

Descend steeply over rocky ground, still on the summit ridge, to meet the corner of a stone wall. Turn left here to face Great Sugar Loaf and follow a narrow but clear path. It bends shortly left to run parallel to the summit ridge before finally bending right away from it to meet the initial track. Turn right onto it to reach the parking place a few hundred metres away.

Distance: 2.4km / 1.5miles. Ascent: 180m / 600ft. Walking time: 1 hour.

5. GREAT SUGAR LOAF

Great (Big) Sugar Loaf exhibits an almost perfect cone from most directions; it has the classic 'mountain' profile as drawn by generations of artistically-inclined children. To avoid a relentless slog up its uniform and unsubtle slopes, this walk starts low in the village of Kilmacanoge thus concealing the full magnitude of the climb for as long as possible. However, if it's a wide view and not a walk that draws you, start from the car park on Calary (235 119) and follow the multitudes!

Go by car or bus to Kilmacanoge 5km / 3miles south of Bray on the N11. Walk a short distance up the R755, taking the side road left opposite the church. Keep straight on where the side road swings left, and turn right at the house 'Redridge' on the left. Keeping straight on the main track along here, you will pass through a gate between two houses about six minutes beyond 'Redridge'. Beyond this gate, follow a path between stone walls, then out onto open hillside, Rocky Valley below on the right. The path becomes indeterminate and after about 15 minutes from the gate, it joins a bigger path. Going left, pass between stone walls and high gorse to exit from the walls onto a wide track, which you follow for about 150m and then turn left up another track. The summit should be visible from about here and any convenient route (as long as it is upwards!) will lead to it.

Predictably the top of Great Sugar Loaf, 501m, commands a wide array of mountains: Djouce close to the west with the massed hills of the northeast of the range to its left and right, Little Sugar Loaf and Bray Head with the sea behind to the east, and the long stretch of Calary Plateau to the south.

For the return, descend northeast from the summit over heaped rocks (watch your step on the initial, very steep descent). This will take you alongside an obvious gully, at the bottom of which you can turn left onto a path running north close to an old deciduous wood. This path ends on tarmac, which is followed all the way back to the start.

Distance: 6.4km/4miles. Ascent: 420m/1,400ft. Walking time: 2½ hours.

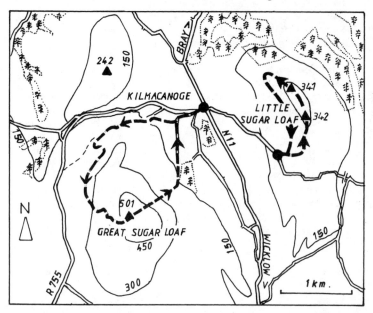

Reference OS Map: Sheet 56 (1:50,000).

6. SEAHAN AND SEEFINGAN

This walk encompasses a long spur of gently rolling but none the less scenic mountains which run from the border of County Wicklow northwest to the suburbs of Dublin, bounded on one side by lowlands and wooded hills and on the other by the glacial valley of Glenasmole.

One of a number of routes by car is as follows. Take the N81 to the roundabout leading to the M50, take the first exit and turn next right. Drive straight ahead for 6.4km/4miles, forking left near the top of a steep hill (this is Stone Cross and there is an appropriate monument to prove it). Continue onward for less than 3.2km/2miles to reach a forest entrance on the left at the crest of the hill (073 201).

Walk the forest track to its end (a deep trench across the track may have to be negotiated — a stream which had been culverted) and here take the rough path on the right upwards to emerge from forest near the shoulder called Ballymorefinn Hill, 525m. Turn right here, forest close on the right and the scenic Glenasmole Reservoirs down on the left. From here it is a simple climb to Seahan over 1km to the south, along a clear track which crosses a wire fence not far from the summit.

Seahan, 648m, commands good views over the northwest of the range, the cairned Seefin to the south being particularly notable. A short descent and shorter ascent (over wet, boggy terrain) ends in the grassy mound of Corrig, 618m, after which southward progress towards Seefingan is along a broad, boggy ridge with the distinct cone of Great Sugar Loaf peeping unmistakably over the anonymous moorland closer at hand.

Seefingan, 724m, is crowned by a huge tumulus and since there is a virtual plateau hereabouts, the tumulus in effect *constitutes* the summit. It is reached by climbing directly from the saddle point between Corrig and Seefingan and veering right at the crest of the hill on a path near the latter. The descent is southwest from this tumulus to reach another substantial tumulus on Seefin, 621m, a summit which, though far from impressive in itself, none the less commands wide views of mountain and plain. From Seefin continue downhill northwest to reach a fence. Keep this closely on the left (be warned: a rifle range is directly to the right!). As you descend a good path develops alongside the fence and forest materialises beyond it.

At length you will reach tarmac. Turn right here and walk along a narrow country road back to the start about 3km away.

Distance: 12km/7.5miles. Ascent: 580m/1,900ft. Walking time: 4½ hours.

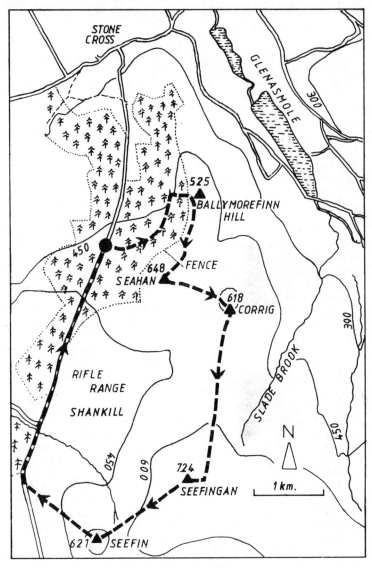

Reference OS Maps: Sheets 50 and 56 (1:50,000).

7. SEEFINGAN, KIPPURE AND CORONATION PLANTATION

This route combines some bleak and austere gently-rolling mountain-side with the more intimate secluded river bank of the youthful River Liffey. The megalithic tombs on Seefin and Seefingan and the TV mast on Kippure exemplify ancient and modern worship customs, and on a severely practical note they are useful landmarks in a fairly blank terrain.

Take the N81 for 2.7km/1.7miles beyond Brittas, turning left here onto the R759. Drive onward on the R759 for 8.8km/5.5miles (after 1.5km/1mile approx. the R759 turns left, signposted Sally Gap) and park in Kippure Wood car park on the left at 080 145. This route is also suitable for cyclists from Dublin.

From the car park follow the track upstream. Do not cross the river where this track descends to a small ford. Veer right and follow a faint path, keeping the forest on your right, and carry on resolutely over fallen trees where the track succumbs. Crossing a fence (carefully) at the edge of mature forest which meets the stream, continue upwards between the stream on the left and young trees on the right. When this is not possible, head into the forest to avoid impediments. Head back to the stream when appropriate. The valley is particularly beautiful. Follow the fence on the left uphill, after the stream has become insignificant, to the corner of the fence. Head directly west, along the ridge on a rough track, to Seefin (*Sui Finn*, Seat of Finn, 621m).

Only at the enormous prehistoric burial chamber on the summit will you fully appreciate your position. West lie the plains of Kildare, while north and south the mountains of the northwest of the range peter out in the low hills on the Kildare border.

Seefingan, 724m, a loftier version of Seefin and like it crowned by a prehistoric grave, is the next target. After it there is a long featureless stretch terminating in Kippure, along the unfortunately unmarked county boundary. Along this stretch you have a choice of views towards Glenasmole to the north or over the Mullaghcleevaun range to the south, though neither direction is particularly exciting.

A soggy mound, unnamed on the maps, followed by a rise through black mud interspersed with startlingly green wedges leads to Kippure (*Cip Iúr*, Yew Mountain, 757m) the highest point in County Dublin. Its TV transmitter is evident, all too evident, for miles around so you will have no difficulty finding the peak, though the surrounding terrain, an inverted pudding bowl, precludes good scenery except in the middle distance and beyond, and even there it is none too inspiring.

The next stage requires careful navigation. Take a compass bearing of about 220° to reach a bridge on the R759 (as you descend, aim for the scattered dark green trees at the eastern extremity of Coronation Plantation). Cross the road and walk down to the River Liffey, here a clear vibrant brook and a far cry from the sluggish, mature river it becomes in the more familiar environment of Dublin.

The homeward stretch starts with a scenic, sometimes marshy walk, keeping close to the right bank of the river. Going downstream, you pass an old house and a bridge and meet a green road which brings you back to the main road about 2km from the start. When I originally wrote the guide you could walk easily beside the river for another kilometre, but with new planting and barbed wire fences, while it is still possible, it cannot be recommended.

Distance: 14.5km/9miles. Ascent: 580m/1,900ft. Walking time: 5 hours.

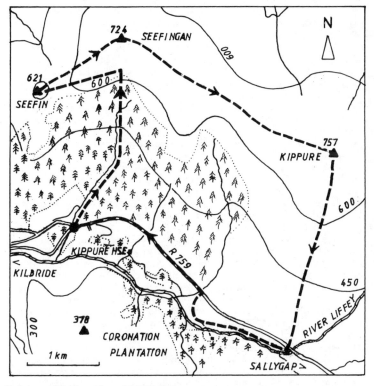

Reference OS Map: Sheet 56 (1:50,000).

8. GLENCULLEN

This walk is hard to title accurately in a word or two. It takes in a little of Glencree, and much of the northeast plateau near Dublin, but the short valley of Glencullen is never far away — hence the title above. Too close to Dublin to escape its litter, unsuitable housing and other eyesores, Glencullen none the less retains a surprisingly rural atmosphere and the mountains to its north and south, though flat to the point of dullness, are sufficiently untamed to escape most of the problems evident lower down.

Take the Shop River variation of the 185 bus route from Enniskerry to its terminus west of Kilmalin (203 172). Decide the most suitable bus route for the Dublin end of the walk beforehand.

Walk west along the road from the terminus for about 2km to the Wicklow Way sign-post at the entrance to Curtlestown Wood. Follow the Way up through the forest and out onto the open ridge. After about 50m leave the Wicklow Way, turning left onto a path (start not obvious) and follow it up to Prince William's Seat, 555m.

On the trek to Glendoo (just under 5km away) follow the ridge northwest. This ridge is so broad that it is easy to wander off it in bad weather; the only easily identifiable point is the tor close to the top of Knocknagun (163 186). All along here the views are quite good, the corries at Lough Bray being particularly noteworthy.

Passing Knocknagun keep along the ditch indicating the Dublin/Wicklow county boundary. Rising towards Glendoo you come to a fence and follow it until it turns west.

From here a forest should be visible about 2km to the north/northwest. Continue northwest across the bog, losing some height, to a depressed marshy area. Keeping this on the right and Cruagh Mountain on the left, head on a walkers' path (if you are lucky enough to find it) to the edge of the forest alongside a stream.

As you reach the forest a clump of trees stands proud of the main forest. Turn left behind these trees and shortly join a path down through the main forest. Follow this.

Turn right onto the forest track below and follow it round a sharp vee. Finally take the first forest track off it — a sharp right — to reach tarmac almost opposite Tibradden car park. The forest terrain hereabouts is quite good of its type, scattered and felled trees giving pleasant glimpses of nearby mountainside.

Cross the road to Tibradden car park, where forest tracks re-commence. Walk to the end of the car park and continue straight on. Turn right at the T-junction and take the first left and first right onto a narrow path. This path ends at a T-junction just out of the forest, where you turn left and find yourself on the western shoulder of Tibradden. Fork right a little further on and walk along the top of the ridge, past a passage grave and granite tor, a route which gives good views south over Glencullen to the ridge traversed earlier in the day.

At the Wicklow Way marker turn left along the Way, following it along the ridge and leaving it to climb Fairy Castle, the highest point around (536m), where the Way turns sharply left. In spite of this, the virtual plateau hereabouts means that the views are circumscribed. Continue east of north downhill to Three Rock which has the dubious distinction of being one of the few unmistakable mountains on this walk — but only because of the numerous masts and blockhouses 'adorning' its summit plateau.

At Three Rock descend north, forest on the left, to a path heading into forest about 500m down from the forest's upper edge. Take this path and descend to the access road for the masts on the summit. Turning right onto it take the next track left into the trees a short distance down. Arriving at surfaced road go right and quickly left onto another track, blocked by large stones, which cuts out a long loop of road. At surfaced road again continue straight downhill to the barrier and out onto Ticknock Road. Going right, walk to the bus; the choice is either left along Kellystown Road to near bus routes that aren't frequent, or straight on to Ballinteer to frequent bus routes that aren't near.

Distance: 21km/13miles. Ascent: 700m/2,300ft. Walking time: 7 hours.

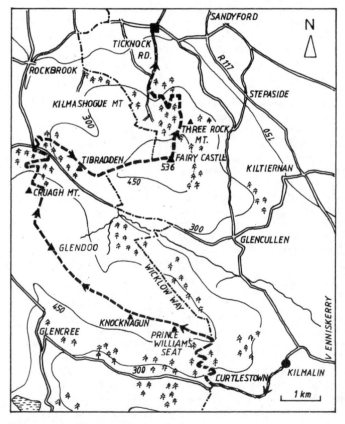

Reference OS Maps: Sheets 50 and 56 (1:50,000).

9. THE TONDUFFS AND MAULIN FROM CRONE

The south side of Glencree is dominated by Maulin. Although, at 570m, not the highest peak around Glencree, it is the most distinctive with its neat cone. To the west, higher and more sprawling, lie Tonduffs North and South, close together in rolling moorland. Then there are the valleys: the rocky slabs of the Raven's Glen, lonely Glensoulan and the Deerpark with the Dargle River falling as the dramatic Powerscourt Waterfall. Although short, the walk offers variety.

Transport must be by car or bicycle. From Enniskerry take the road south, passing Powerscourt Estate on the right and turning right at the T-junction 3.4km/2.1miles from Enniskerry. Park in Crone car park (193 142) on the left 3.9km/2.4miles from this T-junction .

From the car park take the main track. Continue straight at the first junction, passing a map board — the Wicklow Way goes left. Walking west and parallel to Glencree views open up with Knockree in the foreground and the mountains along the Dublin/Wicklow county boundary forming the northern skyline.

At the next junction go right and over a bridge. Cross the stile beside the wooden gate on the left onto a path heading towards the wall on your right. This is the impressive Raven's Glen with its rocky slabs. The path rises alongside the wall, weaving between rocks, heather and gorse.

Approaching the highest point in the wall with a lone bush on a rock about 50m out from it, turn onto a path branching left. It parallels the wall for a short distance and then turns uphill between rocks and heather, easing a little the climb up the rough, lower, steeper slopes of Tonduff North. By the time the path peters out the slope has relented and vegetation become shorter for the long steady pull over easier ground to the top.

A cairn on a peat hag in a desolate lunar-like landscape marks the summit of Tonduff North. Five minutes' walking across almost level ground to the south is Tonduff South (not shown separately on OS Sheet 56), marked by a large rock with a hollow in it — a convenient 'chair' if sometimes damp. Leave Tonduff South, heading southeast, on a path starting very near the summit. This path is clearly defined, veering east, winding amongst peat hags, going over 593m, descending to the col, before reaching firmer ground and finally the top of Maulin. As you walk, the mass of War Hill is on the right across the source of the Dargle River and Glensoulan.

Ascending Maulin (*Malainn*, Hill Brow, 570m) is quite steep on this approach, with the path negotiating a rocky step before the last run up to the summit — an impressive viewpoint.

From here most of the way is downhill. A wide track runs along the eastern shoulder gradually dropping to a wall. Turning right and walking alongside the wall descend into Glensoulan until the Dargle River comes into view below, trees now behind the wall on your left. Watch for a black marker post across the wall — on its other side a yellow arrow directs to a path in the trees and the Wicklow Way back to Crone.

Walking through these trees we have a last short, sharp climb before suddenly exiting onto a high level path along the rim of the Deerpark spread below our feet, pointed Great Sugar Loaf beyond and the Dargle River cascading down the valley head as Powerscourt Waterfall. Deer are sometimes in the mixed woodland bordering the path. The view of the waterfall changes as we progress and it is worth stopping for a final look before the path heads left into the trees. Further down the forest track large, old deciduous trees still stand amongst the relatively more recently planted conifers. Eventually, at a T-junction the Wicklow Way and our route turn right, curve and, back at the map board, turn right again to quickly reach the car park.

Distance: 14.2km/8.8miles. Ascent: 610m/2,000ft. Walking time: 4½ hours.

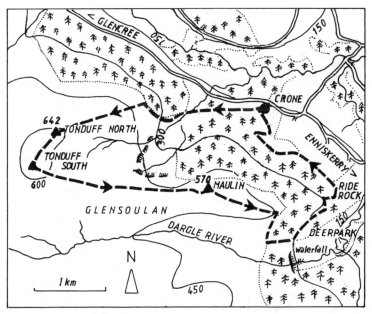

Reference OS Map: Sheet 56 (1:50,000).

10. DJOUCE AND WAR HILL

Djouce is the mountain that dominates the west of the Calary Plateau: a high ridge reaching impressively south to north with a northwestern spur culminating somewhat anticlimactically in War Hill. To the north of these hills secluded Glensoulan carries the upper Dargle River. This route takes in all this scenic and varied terrain in a short but demanding walk.

Drive to Enniskerry and take the road south, passing Powerscourt Gates on the right, towards Roundwood. About 6.1km/3.8miles from Enniskerry, park in the second car park on the right (the first is set back from the road) at Djouce Woods (212 122).

Take the path from the car park downhill to a T-junction, turning left. Shortly there are good views of Powerscourt Waterfall and the Deerpark on the right. Continue downhill to another T-junction, turning left to quickly arrive at the site of Paddock Pond, which was a pleasant reservoir until 1986 when its impounding dam was washed away. Cross the near end, walk along its west side and ascend into the trees beyond it, leaving the forest by crossing a decrepit fence left where feasible.

With forest on the right, ascend to the crest where you will be greeted by a Wicklow Way marker. Follow the Way uphill here towards Djouce, turn right (north, leaving the Wicklow Way) at the crest of the ridge running south from Djouce to White Hill and walk to the summit of Djouce, easily recognisable because of its three rocky outcrops of mica-schist. Djouce (*Dubh ais*, Black Mountain, 725m) has a lofty and somewhat isolated position thus ensuring a wide and varied view of mountain, bogland, plain and even seascape, with nearby Maulin (except for the ubiquitous Great Sugar Loaf) the most easily recognisable peak.

From Djouce push west and then northwest, to the Coffin Stone, as aptly named on the older maps but now replaced by the inappropriate designation 'standing stone' on the newer ones. From here the remainder of the descent and a short ascent ends in War Hill (*An bharr*, the Summit, 686m), a not very elegant mound.

North of War Hill lie the soggy headwaters of the Dargle, riven into the bogland sloping gently downward from the R115 (Military Road). To avoid the worst of this area head northeast from War Hill to the river and follow the right bank through a pleasant, narrow valley downstream to meet forest. Walk uphill for about 500m to a significant indentation in the line of the forest (there is also a Wicklow Way marker at this point). Continue straight ahead uphill for a few more metres, and at the upper end of this indentation cross the fence on the left and follow the track, keeping close to forest on the right. This track shortly turns right to enter forest and widens to a forest track, which is followed all the way down to the site of Paddock Pond.

The final stretch is the same as on the way out. In brief, cross the near end of the former Paddock Pond, turn left and branch right uphill shortly thereafter. The car park is reached by turning right just after an insignificant path on the same side that heads acutely back.

Distance: 15km / 9.3miles. Ascent: 640m / 2,100ft. Walking time: 5¼ hours.

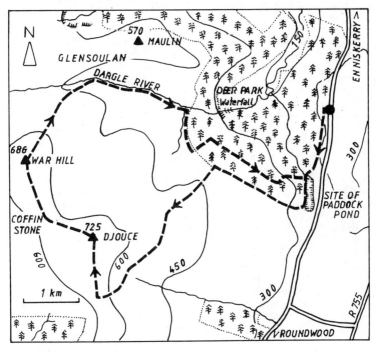

Reference OS Map: Sheet 56 (1:50,000).

11. FANCY, COFFIN STONE AND DJOUCE

This walk might be fancifully described as a 'reverse' sandwich: the tasty meat on the outside with a slice of rather stodgy bread within. The scenic delights of the climb to Fancy yield to the boggy slog to the Coffin Stone. From Djouce on, however, the views are excellent.

Go by car or bus on the N11 to Kilmacanoge, 5km/3miles south of Bray. Turn right onto the R755 here and turn right again onto the R759 after a further 11.3km/7miles. Drive uphill for 3.2km/2miles and park near the large set of gate pillars on the left at 172 064. This is Pier Gates. This walk may also be done using the St Kevin's bus to Roundwood.

From the pillars, walk the tarmacadam road down towards the valley floor along what must be one of the most spectacular motorable roads in the country: the great cliffs under Fancy directly ahead, bumpy Knocknacloghoge to its left and a whole array of lovely mountains around with the purple heathery slopes of the Cloghoge valley close at hand.

At the valley floor cross the first bridge and then, just before a second, turn right up a side track, beside a high wall. Walk a few hundred metres along this track after which you can tackle Fancy (*Fuinnse*, Ash Tree, 595m).

The cliffs of Fancy belie its rather dull top, a heather plateau stretching away to the northwest, but commanding magnificent middle-distance views, prominent among which is the great bulk of Djouce, now to be tackled. To do so head east to a path running parallel and close to the cliffs, turn north onto it and follow it to its end in pathless and very rough country. Continue north through high bracken (in summer), aiming for the stone-cut bridge (Sheepbanks Bridge) over the R759 at 154 095. On the way you will cross the delightful upper Cloghoge River where there are excellent spots for a leisurely lunch.

Cross the R759 at the bridge and walk upstream along the river which the bridge spans, through a desolate, wet moorland towards the Coffin Stone, a prominent heap of stones crowned by a massive boulder which gives the whole assembly its highly appropriate name. On the new OS map, sadly, it is simply called a standing stone.

From the Coffin Stone the ascent to Djouce is easy navigationally, whatever about corporeally; go south uphill and then pick up the line of fence posts and follow it right to the semi-plateau on which Djouce, 725m, stands. The summit is marked by three large outcrops of schist and a trig. point so it is unmistakable and the views predictably magnificent.

The descent is along its southern spur towards White Hill, from which elevated route the Barnacullian ridge to the west, linking the second and third highest peaks in Wicklow (Mullaghcleevaun and Tonelagee), may be seen to perfection.

On this descent you will pick up the Wicklow Way, which you follow going south for the rest of the route. Following a sleeper boardwalk from the forest corner below White Hill the route offers excellent views, best of all when Luggala cliff below Fancy, with Lough Tay tucked in beneath it, is revealed suddenly and dramatically. Hereabouts you will find a memorial stone to J. B. Malone, whose dream of a 'Wicklow Way' eventually came to fruition after nearly twenty years. 'J. B.' was also notable for his weekly articles in the *Evening Herald* which did much to popularise walking in Ireland.

The last stretch is through forest. This would involve complicated directions were it not for the necessarily frequent Wicklow Way markers. Once on the road, the R759 again, turn left and walk first up, then downhill for about 1km to the start.

Distance: 13.7km / 8.5miles. Ascent: 730m / 2,400ft. Walking time: 5½ hours.

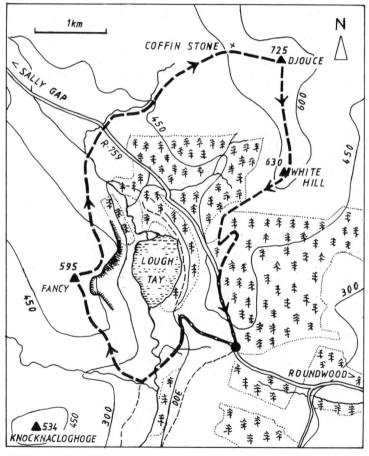

Reference OS Map: Sheet 56 (1:50,000).

12. BALLINRUSH GATES TO LOUGH DAN

Lovely scenery, an undemanding walk, secluded places to picnic and swim — just the formula to transform a sultry summer day into something memorable. This short walk, demanding little effort, takes in some of the best of Wicklow's scenery.

Take the N11 by car to Kilmacanoge, 5km/3miles south of Bray. Turn right here onto the R755 and turn right again onto the R759 after a further 11.3km/7miles. Drive uphill for 3.2km/2miles and park near the gateway on the left marked 'Ballinrush'. This walk may also be done using the St Kevin's bus.

Take the track at the Ballinrush gateway all the way down to the bank of the Cloghoge River opposite the two-storey house at Lough Dan 3km away. This is a really lovely walk, an interplay of rugged mountain, valley and lake. The steady descent means that the shoulders of the nearer mountains eventually hide the summits — but little matter. Near the lake private property blocks further progress. Turn right here down a narrow path and head for the river and the two-storey house where there are places to eat and rest (you may have difficulty justifying the latter to yourself). If you potter round a little you'll find places to swim, but avoid private property.

Time to return. Start back the way you came but once back on the track and just before the first 'summer residence' on the right, turn onto a grassy track heading steeply upwards (you will soon note that the seemingly meagre drop on the outward journey is more than compensated for by the comparatively horrendous rise on the return). A short distance up go left where the track forks and continue upwards to pass ruins on the left and through a gate. Turn right uphill to the forest corner and climb upwards with the trees on the right as far as an obvious entrance to the forest about half way up with a heathery track heading away left. Follow this track which takes you to a gate set high on the horizon.

Cross the gate and turn left with forest directly on the left. Continue straight ahead on a firebreak, keeping the fence on the left and ignoring an extraction track to the right, to descend to a dip where the bend of a forest track on the right comes close to the fence. Turn left onto this track (at the time of writing it is the Wicklow Way), going left at the first junction and continuing straight to reach the road close to Ballinrush gates which are to the left around the bend.

Distance: 6.4km/4miles. Ascent: 280m/910ft. Walking time: 2½ hours.

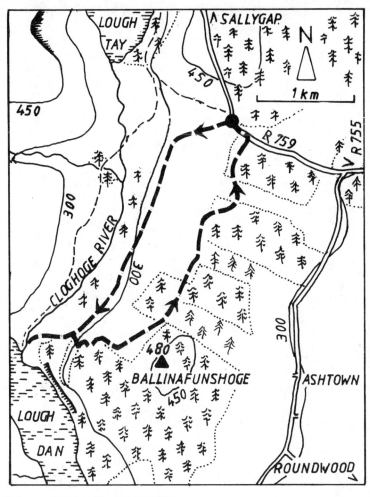

Reference OS Map: Sheet 56 (1:50,000).

13. SCARR AND KNOCKNACLOGHOGE FROM OLDBRIDGE

Scarr is at the centre of one of the most shapely mountain areas in Wicklow. Itself a grassy up-and-down ridge running north and south, it sends three broad, grassy spurs out towards the east and a delightful rocky, hummocky ridge, Kanturk Mountain, running in a wide crescent towards the north. North of Kanturk is the narrow, flat trough of the Inchavore River and northwards again looms rocky Knocknacloghoge, somewhat overshadowed by its higher southern neighbour. Add to this the sylvan valley of the Cloghoge River and the result is one of the most delightful walking areas in the Wicklow Mountains. After heavy rain the rivers on this walk may be difficult to cross.

This is a route which may be conveniently undertaken by St Kevin's bus to Roundwood. Check times for the return before you start! By car drive to Roundwood on the R755, follow signs here towards Lough Dan and park on a grassy patch on the left at Oldbridge (158 017) 3.8km/2.3miles from Roundwood.

From Oldbridge walk north for a few minutes to the first turn on the left, a stony track. Follow it for about 1.3km passing through a gate and forking right after bends to reach a large rectangular clearing in the forest on the left. Walk along two sides of the clearing, keeping forest on your left, to a short clear firebreak which, after crossing the fence, leads to open mountain. Walk the firebreak and when over the fence you find yourself on the northernmost of the three spurs leading to the summit of Scarr. The climb is straightforward and steady — keeping slightly to the right gives a better view of Lough Dan.

The summit of Scarr (*Sceir* or *Scor*, Sharp Rock, 641m) is uncairned but the series of little grassy mounds forming the top is unmistakable. The views of the Barnacullian ridge to the west are particularly fine, especially after rain when the tributaries of the Glenmacnass River cascade down the steep-sided slopes into the glen below.

From the top of Scarr, walk northwest on a distinct path to cross a rickety fence leading to a broad ridge. Descending off this ridge Glenmacnass Waterfall comes into view on your left. If you need reassurance that you are on course you may come across a roughly hewn pillar about 200m beyond the descent. Continue northwards to the area of hummocks, Kanturk, already described. The problem now is to find the firebreak which runs directly down to the copse on the Inchavore River at 133 047. Descend north through high heather and over rough ground to meet a rough track bounding forestry, turn right onto it and within a few metres of its end take the firebreak directly downhill to near the copse. Take great care on this section as there are numerous deep holes concealed in the long grass and heather.

The copse is a delightful spot. The shady oaks and the deep pools of the stream make an ideal place for a well-deserved rest. After that let's hope you have sufficient energy to tackle Knocknacloghoge. Cross the river at the copse and, keeping the forest fence on the left, head towards the summit.

Knocknacloghoge (*Cloghog*, Stony Land, 534m) has a small neat cairn set on a jagged rocky summit. The views of Lough Dan and back to Scarr are particularly fine.

North of Knocknacloghoge, head directly and steeply over rough heather to the Cloghoge Brook, ignoring tempting paths. Once on the far side walk downstream. If the weather is hot, leave time to bathe at a delectable spot further down the brook. A little below this pool and still on the left bank pick up a track, take it to the main track, turn left and head up to the R759 at Pier Gates. This involves a punishing 180m climb, not exactly an inviting prospect towards the end of the day.

From Pier Gates follow Walk 14 and the Wicklow Way back to Oldbridge or Roundwood.

Distance: 19.3km/12miles. Ascent: 970m/3,200ft. Walking time: 7½ hours.

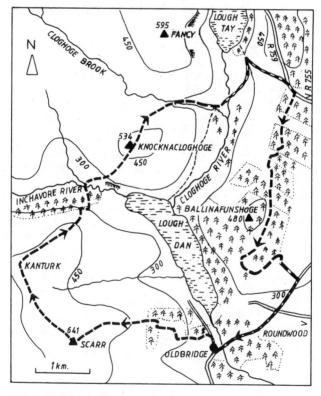

Reference OS Map: Sheet 56 (1:50,000).

14. EASY CIRCUIT OF LOUGH DAN

If you want an easy day in lovely surroundings without climbing any mountains you could do worse, in truth you could hardly do better, than take this variation on Walk 13 along the western end of Lough Dan and finish as in Walk 13 on the Wicklow Way. A beautiful walk.

Transport is as in Walk 13.

From Oldbridge walk northeast along tarmac for about 1.8km, to where the road swings left after a bridge and deteriorates to gravel. Cross a stile beside a gate and after about 50m go through a wicket gate on the right directly opposite 'Carrigeen Lodge' and follow a fenced path parallel to the shore below on the right. Turn right where the path joins a track and continue onwards. Walk along the edge of grassy fields on the valley floor, with the rocky cliffs of Knocknacloghoge beyond on the right, to the oak copse further upstream.

Cross the river here and head downstream and along the lake shore to the two-storey house at the outlet of the Cloghoge River into Lough Dan. The valley traversed beyond the house must be one of the loveliest in Wicklow: Knocknacloghoge rising on the left, wooded Sleamaine on the right and the neat fields of the glen between. The track up the valley crosses the river and climbs up steeply past the cottage at the Luggala Lodge entrance and on to the R759 at Pier Gates.

Turn right onto the R759 and walk about 400m along the road and around the bend to a Wicklow Way marker leading into forest. The next 4km is along the Way on the eastern flank of the Sleamaine–Ballinafunshoge ridge, a high-level (or perhaps better described as 'high but level') route along forest tracks through a pleasant mixture of mature, cleared and new forest and heathery moorland. After a viewpoint over Lough Dan, the Way continues east on a forest track and then descends northeast along a lane between fields to tarmac. Turn right here. Walk the 2km back to the car at Oldbridge or turn left at the next crossroads for Roundwood, 2.5km away. By the time you walk this section of the Wicklow Way it is possible it may be re-directed, if so please follow the markers.

Distance: 16km/10miles. Ascent: 410m/1,360ft. Walking time: 5 hours.

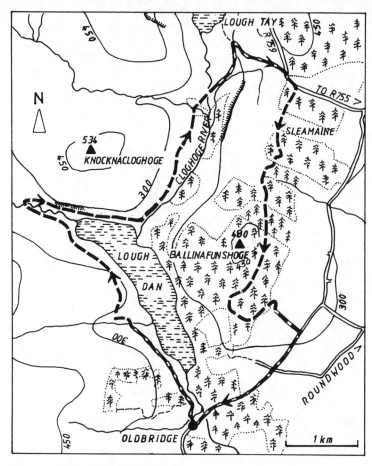

Reference OS Map: Sheet 56 (1:50,000).

15. CIRCUIT OF GLENBRIDE

Wicklow is seen here in its quintessence. Bleak, rolling moorland, decaying and extant peat hags and, mercifully and unusually, an unforested terrain all make for a landscape which is Wicklow at what is normally considered its purest and most typical. None the less, this is not all gentle slopes. The climb of Mullaghcleevaun, Wicklow's second highest mountain, gives a focus and goal to the day's endeavours. A note of warning: the forest shown to the top of Silsean on OS Sheet 56 was not planted at the time of writing.

Car only. Turn onto the R756 from the N81 11.3km/7miles south of Blessington. Drive a further 12km/7.5miles and cross Ballinagee Bridge. Park at the forest entrance on the left of the road just beyond the bridge at 037 023.

Walk along the forest track, forking left after just over 100m and continue for about 1.7km until the track bends right. Take an indistinct path on the left beside the first clump of older trees. Wind between younger trees to the forest fence where two stones provide a crossing place. (If more mature trees come close on each side of the track and it bends right again, you have missed the path. Should you not find it, follow the forest track to a junction, turn left and leave the forest by the gate.) Glenbride is spread before you with its small hamlet above on the left. Cross Gowlan Brook and walk over open moorland to reach Ballinagee River about 100m beyond an isolated tree at the corner of the field walls on the opposite bank. Go upstream to a suitable crossing place, then follow the spur northwest to the top of Silsean (*Soillsean*, Place of Lights, 698m). 'Place of lights' perhaps, but not much to identify the summit, a plateau of wet bogland interspersed with an occasional shallow lakelet.

The shallow gap towards Moanbane is a relatively good place for a rest and food — shelter is even more scarce further on. The short rise to Moanbane (*Moin Bhan*, White Bog, 703m) is a mirror image of the descent from Silsean. In bad visibility the walker unfamiliar with the terrain might be forgiven for supposing that he is back at Silsean, so similar is the summit plateau.

Beyond Moanbane is Billy Byrne's Gap, a region of austere, wet, windswept bogland which yields in turn to steep, drier ground towards Mullaghcleevaun itself.

Mullaghcleevaun (*Mullach Cliabhain*, Summit of the Basket i.e. corrie, 849m) stands at the centre of peaks and offers good views but, mainly because of the gentle slopes around, not as good as its height would suggest. Near the summit cairn and close to the steep dip sweeping down to Cleevaun Lough is a memorial to three An Oige members who perished in a boating tragedy at Clogherhead in the 1950s.

Take especial care on the descent from Mullaghcleevaun: two broad similar spurs run roughly south, one slightly east of south, the other slightly west. Remember, the spur west of south is the correct one. Follow this spur to reach Glasnagollum Brook at about the 400m contour and just below the small gorge. Once across the Brook a deer path heads south contouring towards the forest. Abandon the path round about where it starts to peter out and head for the gate in the forest fence which should now be visible. Stepping stones here take you back over Gowlan Brook.

Walk the forest track beyond the gate and pass a track on the right, then another on the left. After about 2km you reach the junction where you forked left on the outward journey. Keep straight for just over 100m back to the road and car.

Distance: 16.5km/10.5miles. Ascent: 710m/2,350ft. Walking time: 6 hours.

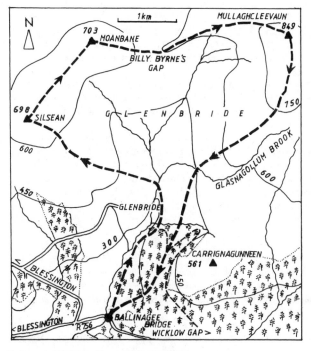

Reference OS Map: Sheet 56 (1:50,000).

16. LUGNAGUN, SORREL AND BLACK HILL

The broad expanse of Pollaphuca Reservoir is never far away on this walk, white against blue reflecting scudding clouds, or leaden grey surfaces producing an effect of mourning heightened by the steady drizzle of the 'soft' day. The mountains adjoining the reservoir are gently sloped and therefore wet but afforestation has not yet laid its monotonous green carpet on a landscape which still faithfully reflects the season's changes.

Because of the difficulty of finding easy routes down to the road running along the east side of Pollaphuca Reservoir, it is necessary to make this an A to B walk. Drive to Blessington on the N81, turn left (east) in the town and drive nearly to Ballyknockan, parking one car in the large car park on the left just before the village (011 073). Drive another car back through Lackan, parking about 2.4km/1.5miles further west at a cul-de-sac road on the right (993 124).

Walk up the cul-de-sac road taking the forest track left at the fork about 1km up. After approx. another kilometre turn left to follow a wide firebreak uphill across two forest tracks and onto open ground near the top of Lugnagun, a nebulous peak which may be ignored. Turn right once out of forest to face Sorrel (*Samhradh*, Hill of Summer?, 599m) the large bare mound to the east, following a path and later an earth bank towards the summit.

Sorrel has a large cairn standing on a plateau of strewn granite rocks. The views towards Pollaphuca Reservoir are excellent; Mullaghcleevaun towers formidably to the south with Black Hill rising more modestly closer to hand across Ballynultagh Gap.

It is Black Hill which is the next goal. Descend over rough heather southwards to Ballynultagh Gap, cross the road at the car park and start the ascent along the bog road, a road shamefully disfigured by several dumps. The road expires near the summit and the walker must carry on to the featureless rounded top of Black Hill, 602m, the summit marked by a very small cairn.

Push on south towards the headwaters of Ballystockan (Cock) Brook, cross it and walk downstream for roughly 1km. About here contour initially southwest away from the brook across indeterminate rough terrain, keeping upland fields (and the scenic Pollaphuca Reservoir) on the right and the shoulder of Moanbane on the left. When the prominent quarry workings at Ballyknockan are close at hand and directly ahead, walk down through several fields, crossing at least one fence, to gain the car park.

Distance: 13km/8miles. Ascent: 550m/1,800ft. Walking time: 4¾ hours.

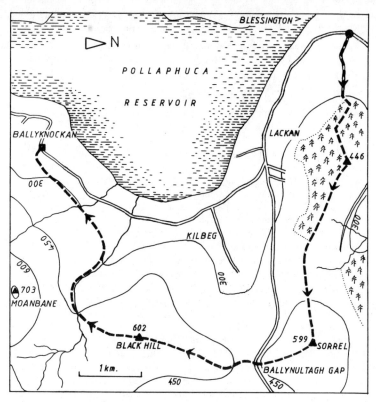

Reference OS Map: Sheet 56 (1:50,000).

17. MULLAGHCLEEVAUN AND TONELAGEE

The second and third highest mountains in Wicklow, Mullaghcleevaun and Tonelagee, are linked by a broad undulating ridge never dipping below 600m, riven in some parts by deeply fissured bogland and covered in other parts by flat areas of sticky, black mud. Indeed the only really firm terrain on this walk is the short grass north and east of Tonelagee. The panorama around it and particularly down onto the steep corrie of heart-shaped Lough Ouler is magnificent and forms a fitting climax to the day's walk.

Park in the small car park on the right (west) of the Military Road R115 at 101 050 about 9km/5.6 miles south of Sally Gap. There is space for only a few cars here but more can be parked in the forest entrance on the left (east), a few hundred metres north. If you have two cars, one may be parked in Glenmacnass car park on the right, nearly 3.2km/2miles south along the Military Road, thus avoiding a road walk at the end of the day.

From the car park climb the right side of Carrigshouk, 571m, on an intermittent path, avoiding the steep slabs of the direct approach. The summit of Carrigshouk may be bypassed and Mullaghcleevaun East Top tackled directly over featureless terrain. East Top, 795m, has a small cairn and a more impressive heap of boulders which looks as though it is artfully arranged to form a modern sculpture. Beyond the East Top a sea of oozy bog confronts the walker intent on a direct approach; a prudent tack to starboard (right) is advisable.

Mullaghcleevaun, 849m, is described under Walk 15; enough to say that the trig. pillar and memorial plaque are sufficient identification. Take the ridge southwards (with the slightest hint of east) along the Barnacullian ridge here, at the headwaters of the Glenmacnass River, rent by deep fissures which make for tortuous progress. If you wish to avoid sticky mud further on keep to the east of the ridge.

South of Barnacullian the ground is better — rough grass and moorland. A gentle drop is followed by a distinct rise to Stoney Top. Head south from Stoney Top to confront the steep rise to Tonelagee close by, watching out, in cloud, for the grassy cliffs above Lough Ouler to the east. Tonelagee (*Toin le gaoth*, Backside to the Wind, 817m) is an impressive viewpoint, far more commanding than the somewhat higher Mullaghcleevaun. The waters of Turlough Hill are visible to the south with the entire Lugnaquilla massif to its right. Scarr and the other mountains around Lough Dan dominate the east with a bumpy skyline. Add to this the great corrie of Lough Ouler, soon to be encountered on the descent, and the remaining pains of the ascent will soon be forgotten.

The rock-strewn descent along the south side of Lough Ouler is navigationally straightforward. Beyond the lake featureless moorland warrants a compass bearing directly to Glenmacnass car park. To avoid wet feet it may be worthwhile diverting about 70m upstream of the car park where there are natural stepping stones. Turn left and walk left along the road to the start unless you have a car here. A footbridge was erected about 800m upstream of the car park but washed away by floods. It may be replaced sometime.

Assuming two cars:
Distance: 13.7km/8.5miles. Ascent: 700m/2,300ft. Walking time: 5½ hours.

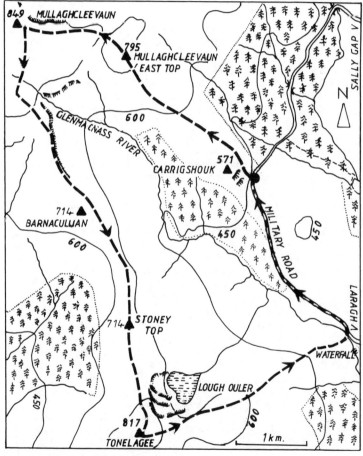

Reference OS Map: Sheet 56 (1:50,000).

18. FAIR MOUNTAIN AND LOUGH FIRRIB

The region south of the Wicklow Gap road (the R756) is a high, wide, desolate moorland without notable landmarks. It is therefore an ideal area for the aspiring navigator to try out his or her skills, indeed not only to try them out but have them rigorously examined. The reward for success is the satisfaction of finding one's way between small and secluded features on a bleak moorland. The penalty for failure might be hours of tiring trudging over endless peat hags — but let's not even think about that!

Car only. Turn onto the R756 from the N81 11.3km/7miles south of Blessington. Drive a further 12km/7.5miles, turning right through a gate onto a forest track. (Watch out carefully for it!) Drive 0.5km/0.3mile further and park near the bridge at 033 020.

Take the forest track past the forest bar and follow it and, alas, the huge Turlough Hill electricity pylons, to the first hairpin bend, a right. Here look out carefully on the left for a narrow but clear path heading into forest. After about six minutes walking it peters out. Bear left through a muddy semi-firebreak and after another five minutes emerge from the trees. On the left is a heathery rocky knoll. Climb upwards towards a fence on the left.

Cross the fence just beyond the boulders and turn left (east). With the fence as a guide you can now relax from navigational concerns for a while and admire the scenery, primarily north towards Tonelagee across the Wicklow Gap. You will also notice a new forest track running parallel to the fence a short distance away. As you advance, and Fair Mountain, with huge boulders along its flank comes into view, turn southwards across the heather towards a col. Cross the stream and ascend Fair Mountain by the easier sloping ground.

The views from the summit of Fair Mountain, 569m, are little better than those from lower down, Tonelagee still the major natural feature. What is new is a major man-made feature, the ramparts of the top reservoir of Turlough Hill. And it is on these ramparts that attention must now focus. Head southeast from Fair Mountain, pick up a short stretch of tarmac near the reservoir and, at the level ground above, face Lough Firrib.

Lough Firrib is tiny: snugly hidden among undulating moorland it is far from easy to find. You may be lucky and pick up a trench or a set of bootprints (hardly a path) which runs to the lough or you may choose self-reliance and the compass. Either way Lough Firrib is a good place to rest and eat, and to prepare for the next stage, the leg to Art's Cross.

Art's Cross (038 991) is, slightly surprisingly, actually a wooden cross set above steep ground overlooking Glenreemore. On clear days, when you don't need it for navigation, it is visible for miles; on bad days, when you do, you won't see it unless you bump against it. Such are the trials of the hill-walker.

From Art's Cross you can drop into Glenreemore but if you wish to retain wide views, keep high by heading over open ground into the vee formed by the Glenreemore and Asbawn Brooks, cross right over the former and walk downstream through wet ground between two forests to the electricity pylons at the 'cul' of a cul-de-sac road.

From here to the start it is 'simply' a matter of continuing to follow the Glenreemore Brook downstream to its junction with the Kings River and then following the Kings upstream. 'Simple' navigationally but some tough, wet terrain makes for slow progress, in particular at the junction where young conifers are planted. After this, underfoot conditions gradually improve and you can enjoy a pleasant riverside walk, a walk whose attractions will be enhanced if you are lucky enough to catch sight of a heron fishing among the boulders of the river.

Distance: 13.7km/8.5miles. Ascent 480m/1,600ft. Walking time: 4½ hours.

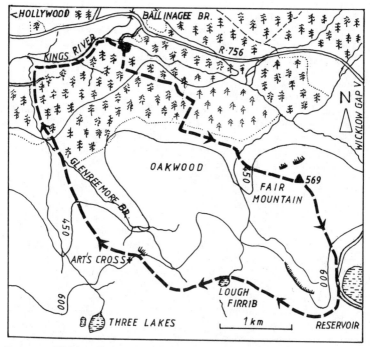

Reference OS Map: Sheet 56 (1:50,000).

19. THREE LAKES AND ART'S CROSS

This is an area where the next peat hag to be surmounted, or the nearest stretch of dull, rolling moorland to be trudged, limits visibility to a few soggy square yards. Nevertheless the sudden unexpected glimpses of Moanbane or Tonelagee looming across the Wicklow Gap and the satisfaction of finding the next insignificant landmark in a well-nigh featureless area make this walk rewarding. Don't attempt it in bad visibility unless you are very sure of your navigational skills!

Car only. Turn onto the R756 from the N81 11.3km/7miles south of Blessington. Drive for a further 8km/5miles to Granabeg (004 021), a hamlet whose most notable feature is the old schoolhouse on the right (south) of the road.

Starting at the near side of the schoolhouse, walk south down a path through fields to the Kings River, cross it by a metal bridge and ascend the south bank to tarmac. Note where you reached the road — you will need this information for the return. Turn right and take the forest track into the forest on the left. This track climbs upwards in a zigzag manner and after about 20 minutes emerges onto apparently open ground where there is a young plantation. There is another forest a short distance ahead. Follow the track through it and emerge onto open mountain. Climb upwards, continuing alongside the trees. After a short distance the southern boundary of the forest is reached. Head south for the top of Round Hill at 003 995, marked 511m on OS Sheet 56.

From here to Lough Firrib your route is punctuated by a series of obscure landmarks not *all* of which you need find, though it will certainly add to your peace of mind if you do. Round Hill is a gently-sloping spur distinguished by a few stones, an unusual feature in an area of bogland. Then the bend in the boundary ditch climbing Table Mountain at about Point 599m, Three Lakes (in spite of the name there are only two), the wooden Art's Cross at 038 991 and finally Lough Firrib. A not very prominent series of goals set in ubiquitous moorland to save you (literally) from a sticky end.

From Lough Firrib you can take the high route over the spur to the north or the low route down into Glenreemore, depending on the day and your inclination. Let's assume a descent into Glenreemore (the high route is described in Walk 18). Head directly northwest over fairly steep ground into a delightful pocket at the headwaters of the Glenreemore Brook. (Look out among the rocky slabs on the left for the plaque to Art O'Neill.) Wander down the right bank, past the incoming tributary of the Asbawn Brook and into a wide gap between two plantations (this gap is not indicated on the maps). Cross the bridge just beyond the power lines and turn left onto tarmac. A little over 1.5km west on tarmac, turn right for the metal bridge and the car.

Distance: 16.5km / 10.5miles. Ascent: 500m / 1,660ft. Walking time: 5½ hours.

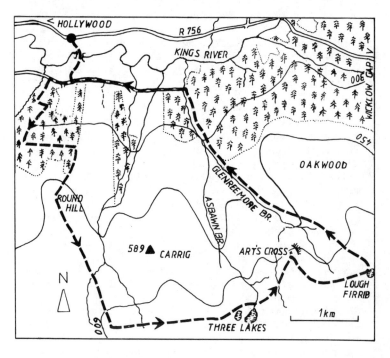

Reference OS Map: Sheet 56 (1:50,000).

20. THE SPINK AND THE DERRYBAWN RIDGE

The wooded Spink rears impressively over the eastern end of the Upper Lake at Glendalough and runs from there along its southern shore in a line of sheer cliffs occasionally indented by rocky bluffs. After an impressive start along the Spink the route takes us to grassy, gently sloped Mullacor and down narrow Derrybawn, a rib of metamorphic rock and the finest ridge in Wicklow. A short but memorable walk.

Drive to the upper car park, Glendalough (111 964) about 1.5km/1mile beyond the Royal Hotel Glendalough. Or take St Kevin's bus to the Glendalough terminus. Travellers by bus should walk into the cemetery containing the Round Tower, cross the bridge at the far end, turn right and walk the 1.5km or so to the start proper.

Leave the car park at the southwestern corner and walk south to the small information office (open during the summer months only). Turning right, shortly cross the bridge and climb up the steps by the foaming Pollanass Waterfall to the forest track above and at the multiple junction turn sharply right uphill.

Stay on this track around the first bend, passing a notice warning of dangerous cliffs. About 1.5km from the bend go right where the track forks and 50m beyond, where larger and smaller trees meet, a ride line heads uphill to the right. The first sight from the crest of the Spink is breathtaking — the Upper Lake seemingly at your feet with the valley of Glendalough stretching beyond it, the great cliffs of Camaderry opposite and the Glenealo valley reaching west into the mountains. It is a marvellous panorama.

Turn left to climb the rocky steps. Walk parallel to the valley below at first, then veering southwest as a forest track provides easier walking, though still uphill. (To dispel niggling doubts about your location you should note that the OS map simplifies the boundary of the forest on the left — it is actually very ragged. Nor, understandably, does it depict the huge clear-felled areas of forest.)

Follow the fence on your left, your walk over Mullacor and Derrybawn coming into view to the southeast and east as you turn south with the fence. Near the saddle between Lugduff and Mullacor you cross the line of the fence and lose a little height descending to the pass, then climb steeply up Mullacor (*Mullach mhor*, Great Summit, 657m). The summit commands fine views especially towards the Lugnaquilla massif. On the descent east a boggy path follows the centre of the ridge, trees coming into view on the left as you approach a fence and the corner of the forest. Cross a stile at the southern corner of the fence and head northeast for the start of the bumpy Derrybawn ridge. The views along here, especially towards the Upper Lake, are excellent and a path, much of it on rock, leads you out along the ridge which slopes sharply away on both sides. From the cairn on Derrybawn Mountain continue straight ahead for a short distance down onto a small saddle from which a path drops steeply to the left, heading towards a vee at the lowest point of the forest edge below. (Here we might note that though the remainder of the walk is in forest, the trees are mature and well spaced and the views through them excellent.) Cross the stile at this vee and continue on the path to turn right onto the first forest track, the Wicklow Way. Keeping on the Way take the first turn left and then, to provide a slightly different perspective from the outward journey, take the first right (it is just before the first of two bridges). This track zigzags downhill to the valley floor with Pollanass Waterfall on the left. Here a left takes you back to the small information office and the car park, while the bus is to the right.

While you are at Glendalough, it would be a pity (if you don't already know them) not to visit the monastic ruins below the Lower Lake. The Visitor Centre at the lower car park is also well worth a visit.

Distance: 12km / 7.5miles. Ascent: 630m / 2,080ft. Walking time: 4½ hours.

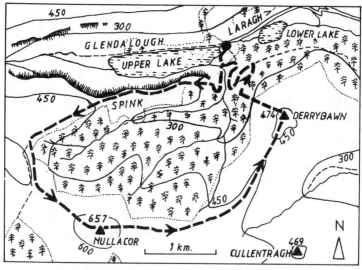

Reference OS Map: Sheet 56 (1:50,000).

21. GLENEALO, TURLOUGH HILL AND CAMADERRY

The view west up the Upper Lake in Glendalough towards Glenealo is magnificent, seen by countless thousands of day-trippers annually and captured on hundreds of photos and drawings. But what about the view from Glenealo east towards Glendalough? It is equally good (probably better) but is seen and enjoyed only by the hardy souls who ascend the zigzags terminating the western end of Glendalough. Add to this Camaderry, the great wedge of mountain lying between Glendalough and Glendasan, and the ingredients are those of a most enjoyable walk.

Start at the upper car park, Glendalough (111 964). Directions are given under Walk 20.

From the car park join the throngs (on Sundays anyway) strolling along the shores of the Upper Lake. Beyond its end, thread a way through the old lead mine workings. While these are not a thing of beauty and certainly promise to be an eyesore forever, they are interesting geologically. They stand on a metamorphic zone between the granite further west and the ancient Ordovician strata to the east which were thrust aside by the up-swelling granite. Similar workings occur in Glendasan and Glenmalure, all three along this zone.

Ascending the zigzags you will find some excellent resting and swimming places along the river on the left; they are especially good higher up. (On hot days better take a solemn vow before you stop that you won't abort the walk!) The scenery is not quite so good on the fairly level ground in Glenealo and you can concentrate on pleasant, though wet, walking along the left (true) bank of the river.

Continue up the valley taking the main stream rather than tributaries and at the soggy headwaters climb the remaining distance to the level ground between tiny Lough Firrib and the gigantic sloping sides of Turlough Hill Reservoir. Thanking your lucky stars that you have to find the latter rather than the former, walk round the southern perimeter fence of the reservoir, negotiate the peat hags beyond and ascend Camaderry (*Ceim a' doire*, Pass of the Oakwood, 698m) which has a rather flat top thus making the cairn particularly useful. There is a lower second peak of Camaderry to the southeast, after which a good path gives easy walking right down the spur between Glendasan on the left and Glendalough on the right, a long easy descent with lovely views.

You can cut the walk short by descending a steep path right to the upper car park, but if you have the time why should you? Instead continue down the spur, keeping on top rather than being tempted down to the right, pick up a forest track near the end and turn left onto it. It will guide you back on a boomerang's progress high above the shore of the Lower

Lake and then gently to earth near the eastern shore of the Upper Lake, crossing the direct descent via the steep path, to end what should have been an enjoyable day.

Distance: 14.5km/9miles. Ascent: 610m/2,000ft. Walking time: 5 hours.

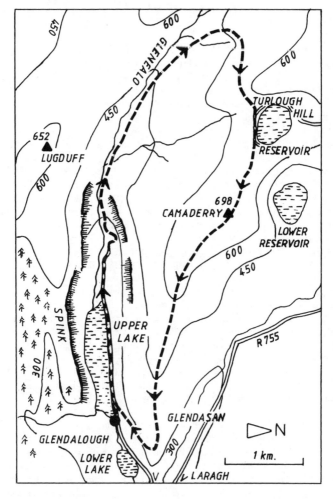

Reference OS Map: Sheet 56 (1:50,000).

22. CARRIGLINNEEN AND MULLACOR

Carriglinneen is a small but craggy peak and the initial climb from its south side is stiff but satisfying. You next cross the Military Road where the peaks are rounded and a trifle bland but give extensive panoramas. The walk ends with a section of the Wicklow Way offering excellent views down into Glenmalure.

By car drive 1.4km/0.9mile south of Laragh on the R755, turning right sharply uphill here for Glenmalure. Drive on for another 8km/5miles to Drumgoff crossroads (107 909), turn left and park immediately on the right at Glenmalure Lodge, well placed for refreshments after your walk.

From the crossroads walk southeast along the road towards Rathdrum. After about 1km take a tarmac road, marked cul-de-sac, on the left. The road winds upwards for 1.5km to where the tarmac runs out, with farm buildings on the right and a narrow tarmac road to a private house on the left. Go through a pair of gates straight ahead and onto a track. Just through the gates turn left and head up through the bracken for a 150m climb to Carriglinneen (*?Carraig glinnin*, Rock of the Little Glen, 455m). If the bracken is too high for a direct ascent you can continue on the track to the highest point and turn left onto a narrow track and then path to the summit and return the same way. Alternatively if you prefer to avoid Carriglinneen stay on the track.

The summit is indistinct but the next stretch northeast along the high ground parallel to the Military Road is clear enough. If you have taken the direct ascent from the track below follow a path which widens to a narrow track, and which eventually joins a wide track heading to the highest point on tarmac between Laragh and Glenmalure.

Cross the road (the appropriately located memorial to the cyclist Shay Elliot near the top of the hill is worth the slight detour) and take the forest road on the other side. The rule from here on as far as Mullacor is to keep straight on regardless; walk (in turn) on a good track, a narrow track, a path with an accompanying ditch and fence and finally open terrain, on the way bypassing Cullentragh. Beyond Cullentragh watch out on the right for the Derrybawn ridge bumping northwards on its rocky route towards Glendalough.

Mullacor, 657m, is an excellent location for long views and the steep drop to be walked west beyond it renders it unmistakable if only in retrospect — its eminence is not particularly evident from the southeast.

At the end of this drop, turn left on a path towards forest, and meet a Wicklow Way post. The Way can now be followed right back to the start. Running first parallel to the forest, it then plunges down through it, wavers indecisively on a stretch of path to a lower track, then belatedly but resolutely heads straight back southeast above the valley floor, swings left into the side valley containing the Military Road and deposits the walker on tarmac at Coolalingo Bridge. Turn right here and walk the short distance to Drumgoff.

Distance: 16.5km/10.5miles. Ascent: 610m/2,000ft. Walking time: 5¾ hours.

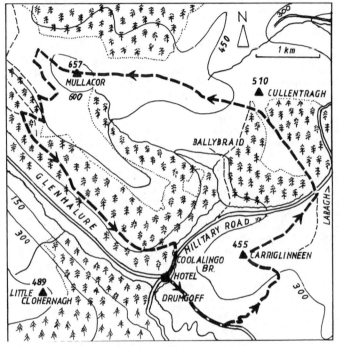

Reference OS Map: Sheet 56 (1:50,000).

23. GLENMALURE, THE FRAUGHAN ROCK GLEN AND LUGNAQUILLA

Probably the most rewarding approach to Lugnaquilla is from Baravore at the head of Glenmalure. A short but steep ascent via a series of tiny valleys culminates in Wicklow's only 900m summit, and is followed by a high-level, easy stroll with stunning views in all directions. A lovely walk.

Car only, though this walk may also be done from Glenmalure Youth Hostel. Take the R755 for 1.4km/0.9mile south of Laragh turning right here steeply uphill towards Glenmalure. Drive for a further 7.2km/4.5miles and turn right here at Drumgoff at the crossroads. Park in the large car park at the head of the valley (066 941) a further 5km/3miles on.

Cross the river by the footbridge and walk on tarmac upstream to just past the youth hostel. Fork left uphill here and walk steadily upwards along a track through forest until it comes close to the river on the left and a forest track comes in from the right. Continue straight on the forest track for about a further kilometre until the track comes close to the river for a second time and starts to deteriorate. Walk through a few trees to the river bank and cross the river above the fences on the opposite bank. Turn right to face up the Fraughan Rock Glen. The scenery from here on is spectacular — and improves as you go on: the far wall of Glenmalure behind, the rugged shoulder of Clohernagh to the left, the great rocky cliffs of Ben Leagh to the right, and ahead the rapids cascading over the steep ground which bounds the glen to the southwest.

Walk to the rapids and then climb parallel to them to a second higher valley, this one generally wet and perhaps a little dull. Climbing the easily surmountable rocky wall behind it reveals a third valley, and when you climb the steep grassy slope behind this, the gently sloped terrain above heralds the summit plateau of Lugnaquilla itself.

The view from the immediate area of the great cairn on Lugnaquilla (*Log na Coille*, Hollow of the Copse, 925m) is dull, a grassy plateau whose pastoral atmosphere is accentuated by grazing sheep. But walk a few yards in any direction and a great panorama is suddenly revealed. The high hills of the range crowd in from all directions: whale-backed Tonelagee and Mullaghcleevaun to the north, Keadeen to the west, the long spur of Clohernagh reaching out to the east, to the southeast the graceful cone of Croaghanmoira, and Mount Leinster, topped by its TV aerial, to the south. A wonderful series of views.

From Lugnaquilla descend a gentle slope to Clohernagh (*Clocharnach*, Stony Place, 800m), a long stretch with wide spectacular views and excellent underfoot conditions. Just two points about the otherwise easy navigation: firstly if you take a direct bearing from the top of Lug to Clohernagh, be prepared at the start to swerve prudently left to avoid the cliffs of the South Prison, and secondly take care to choose the Clohernagh spur (left) rather than the Carrawaystick spur at the one distinct junction.

The summit of Clohernagh barely rises from the general level, so its large cairn is an important landmark, especially as the next left to Art's Lough is a little difficult navigationally. To avoid cliffs on the direct route from the summit, walk about north/northeast for approx. 500m, then swing north and finally northwest to descend on a grassy ramp to the lake.

Art's Lough has a lovely setting: rocky cliffs bounding it on its southwest side, and if you care to walk a little further northwest, giving a lovely view over the Fraughan Rock Glen, up which you toiled earlier.

But alas, back to navigation. The idea now is to reach the high end of the track which reaches tarmac at 079 928 and which extends much further than is shown on the OS map. To do this, cross a fence running into the lake roughly halfway along the northeast shore and follow it to another fence a few metres away and parallel to the lake. Walking left inside the second fence leads to a stile a short distance away. Cross the stile and turn left immediately onto a rough path through heather. (There are two more fences running out of the northwestern end of the lake which should *not* be followed.) This path initially runs parallel to the fence, but then swings away from it to reach the indistinct end of the track (if you lose the path simply head northeast to pick up the track).

Once on the track you can breathe easily. Turning left at the T-junction and ignoring what are obviously minor tracks, follow it down through forest in various stages of growth, which allows glimpses down into Glenmalure and across to the mountains to its north. At length you should cross a forest bridge, beyond which is tarmac. Turn left here to reach the car park less than 2km away.

Distance: 15.3km/9.5miles. Ascent: 800m/2,600ft. Walking time: 5¾ hours.

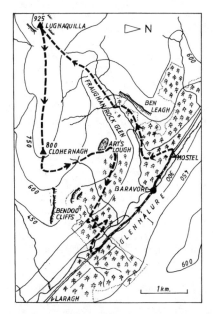

Reference OS Map: Sheet 56 (1:50,000).

24. BALLYBRAID AND MULLACOR

A short walk with some lovely views. A steady rise to Mullacor is followed by a gentle descent along mostly open forest tracks overlooking Glenmalure and the Lugnaquilla massif. The first view of the full extent of Carrawaystick Waterfall is particularly notable.

By car take the R755 for 1.4km/0.9mile south of Laragh. Turn right uphill here and drive for a further 8km/5miles to park at the forest entrance on the right (if you have gone as far as Drumgoff crossroads you have overshot by a few hundred yards).

First you might care to examine Coolalingo Bridge spanning the main road. It is a lovely stone arch — they don't make bridges like that nowadays!

From the forest entrance take the track right (it's the Wicklow Way) but continue straight on where the Way turns left. Follow the track, at first about level, then starting to climb. Ignore a turn to the right and continue around a sharp bend to the left. Take the first turn right, thus heading into Ballybraid with the open land of Cullentragh across on the northern side of the valley and the wooded southeast spur of Mullacor on the southern side.

Near the head of the valley the track swings sharply left away from the forest edge. The first turn right will take you almost to the perimeter fence. Pick your way through a few trees, cross the fence onto open ground and continue upwards, the forest fence initially on the left, then straight on past the end of the forest to the top of Mullacor. Although only a there-and-back, this detour gives excellent views particularly north and south, the directions of prominent peaks.

Retrace your steps to the corner of the forest and turn right along the top edge. Continue downwards, forest on the left until, after about 15 minutes from this corner, your way is blocked by a fence. Stay outside the fence, keeping it on your left, and follow it as it turns left and takes you to a firebreak straight ahead. A definite path leads you along the firebreak and at its end you turn right downhill on a narrower firebreak. Walk through a difficult branch-strewn section in this firebreak, detouring left at one point, before emerging gratefully onto a forest road from where you can study the whole Lugnaquilla massif with the chunky block of Clohernagh to the fore and Carrawaystick Brook cascading vigorously into Glenmalure.

Turn left at this forest road, go right at the fork and turn left at the next decision point (perhaps this would be better described as a 'straight ahead'). This will take you round the southeast spur of Mullacor and high above the side valley carrying the Military Road. Eventually you will reach a sharp bend down to the right and realise that you have rejoined your outward route. Continue downhill, ignoring the turn on the left, to meet the Wicklow Way again and accompany it back to the car.

Distance: 11.1km/6.9miles. Ascent: 520m/1,700ft. Walking time: 4 hours.

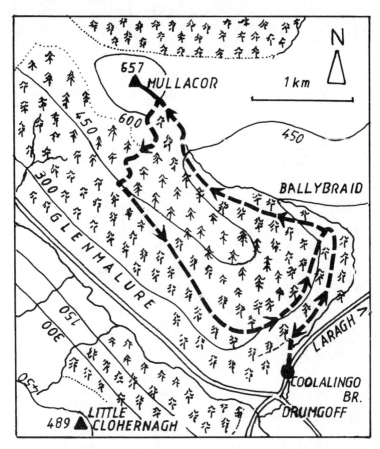

Reference OS Map: Sheet 56 (1:50,000).

25. TABLE MOUNTAIN AND THE LUGDUFFS

The start of this walk is lovely but it is an unchanging loveliness. With the heights attained and a stretch of corrugated bogland behind you the delightful ridge of the Lugduffs beckons, offering magnificent views into Glendalough and towards Lugnaquilla. A steep descent into Glenmalure rounds off what should have been a moderately hard but rewarding day.

Car only. Drive to Drumgoff crossroads (no signpost) about 8.8km/ 5.5miles from Laragh as described under Walk 23, turn right here and drive to the head of the valley, parking in the large car park there at 066 941.

From the car park cross the river and walk upstream on tarmac to the youth hostel. Continue straight ahead on a track beyond it. The gradual ascent of 5km from car park to the top of the pass is easy navigationally — simply keep the river close on the right where a choice is to be made. The views, however, though scenic, especially back into Glenmalure, are a trifle unvarying and not helped by recent forestry developments. It may therefore be with some relief that you reach the pass, still on the same track but a track which now threatens to merge forever into the surrounding country.

The pass is the last comfortable place for eating for some time, so after it you may feel up to tackling the next section, a difficult one navigationally. Head north to Table Mountain, a cairn set on a boggy plateau, and then face Three Lakes (there are actually two) which you don't need to reach in good weather but is a useful landmark in bad. The next goal is Conavalla (*Ceann a' bhealaigh*, Head of the Road, 734m), a post set in peat hags. On leaving Conavalla, to avoid losing height on the trek to Lugduff, walk north/northeast for about 1km and then turn southeast. A steady descent follows over bogland to a col and then on to a great ridge walk.

The ridge is prefaced by a sharp rise, Lugduff West, and a slight drop followed by another rise ending in Lugduff itself (*Log dubh*, Black Hollow, 652m). In bad visibility it is difficult to gauge exactly how far you have progressed along this ridge, so the bright white quartzite stones just before the summit make identification of this point easy. Keep your fingers crossed for good weather though, for the jagged Spink and later the Upper Lake at Glendalough are just two outstanding features in a panorama running superbly from north through east to south.

Lugduff East is an easy climb over short grass, after which head southwest to descend steeply from the ridge towards Glenmalure, forest close on the left. The last stretch of this descent is through gorse and ferns, the latter if high and therefore fly-infested, being well-nigh intolerable in hot humid summer weather. Once on the road, lick your wounds (if sustained), turn right and walk less than 1.5km back to the car.

Distance: 16km/10miles. Ascent: 810m/2,650ft. Walking time: 6 hours.

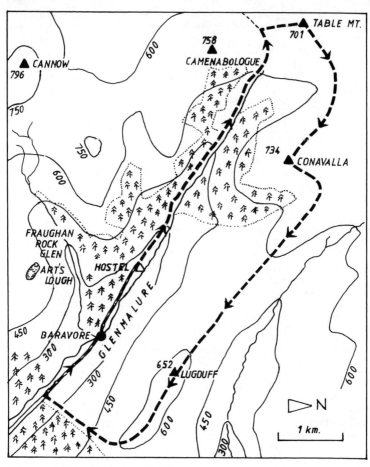

Reference OS Map: Sheet 56 (1:50,000).

26. CARRAWAYSTICK AND CROAGHANMOIRA

Croaghanmoira, with Great Sugar Loaf, is the nearest approach to the classical pyramid-shaped mountain in Wicklow and though Carrawaystick is merely a spur of Lugnaquilla and not really a distinct peak, under it nestles the delectable Kelly's Lough. It is a pity that a rising tide of monotonous conifers swathes the valleys and threatens the solitude of Kelly's Lough itself. Come before it rises even higher!

By car drive to Drumgoff crossroads (107 909) as described under Walk 22.

Walk south past the ruins of the military barracks, turning right after about 300m, thus following the Wicklow Way. Continue on the Way uphill but where it branches left downhill continue straight ahead. Turn first right onto another track and continue steadily upwards to pass between the pillars normally found with a bar at a forest entrance. Just beyond these pillars turn right onto another track and continue, going right at the fork. Where the track reaches a fence and bends sharply right downhill, leave it to walk uphill inside the fence, past a bend left and to a stile. Cross the stile and walk southwest to the corner of Kelly's Lough, an unusually large corrie lake at a high altitude, and a delightful spot for a rest.

From the eastern end of Kelly's Lough climb the steep slope to its south (care should be taken here as in places only a thin coating of vegetation covers very steep rock slabs) to Carrawaystick Mountain (*Ceathramhadh istigh*, Inner Quarter, 676m). Returning to the fence and continuing up along it, although still steep, gives easier walking. No need to find its exact top, though if you do find the small cairn perched precariously on a peat hag, count it a bonus. Another stile on top of the ridge takes you over the fence as the next target you really must find is an angle in a forest fence southeast of Carrawaystick and about 1.5km away, an absolute necessity given the wide tracts of forestry all around. This is easier said than done since the forest has been extended upwards. A compass bearing of 130° will take you to the edge of younger trees. Walk one of the trenches between them down to a forest track. To reach the angle in the fence leave the track at a small cairn at roughly the highest point on the track and at a corner in the forest on the southeastern side of the track. Walk along the edge of the trees, keeping them on your right, to reach the stile and angle in the fence and the wide firebreak which will take you along the northwestern side of Slievemaan.

About 15 minutes walking from the fence and stile take a wide well-defined firebreak on the left, opposite a point on the right where the fence posts change direction slightly rightwards. At the end of this firebreak, turn right onto the forest track, the Wicklow Way, and take it around a sharp bend to the left, leaving it where it turns right onto another forest track. Continue straight until you reach tarmac at the top of the pass between Drumgoff and Aghavannagh.

Most navigational difficulties now behind, you can face the climb to Croaghanmoira with equanimity. Cross the road and follow the path on the opposite side which leads to the obvious forest corner. Once here, cross the fence (with care not to damage it) and continue with forest on your right for a few hundred metres until the path turns sharply left. Follow this path steeply to the summit of Croaghanmoira (*Cruachan maoir*, Hill of the Steward or

Overseer, 664m) which commands excellent views stretching all the way from Great Sugar Loaf to the Blackstairs. Small wonder then that it was a pivotal point for the triangulation of the country in the original survey in the nineteenth century.

From Croaghanmoira retrace your steps to the forest corner and then walk northeast along the Fananierin ridge, a rocky, narrow rib and one of the best such in the range. Fananierin (*Fana an iarainn*, Iron Slope, 426m) at the end of the ridge is not strictly necessary to the route but the views it offers along Glenmalure make it worth the effort.

From here retrace your steps to the lateral stone wall encountered along the ridge and descend half-right to a gate at a break in the forest that stretches along the Military Road. Cross the bridge here, walk through the forest to tarmac, turn right and walk the 2km to Drumgoff.

Distance: 20.5km / 12.8miles. Ascent: 940m / 3,100ft. Walking time: 7½ hours.

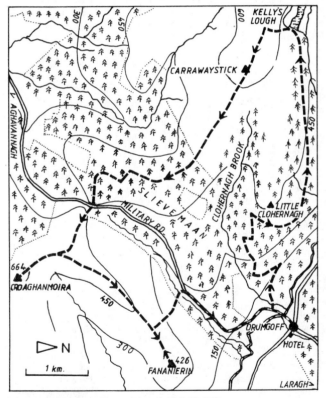

Reference OS Maps: Sheets 56 and 62 (1:50,000).

27. CIRCUIT OF IMAAL

The circuit of Imaal makes a long and rewarding walk taking in a wide array of high mountain scenery and culminating in Lugnaquilla itself. Whether it is better to do it clockwise or anti-clockwise is a toss-up, but anti-clockwise as described below has the advantage of a long scenic descent through magnificent country ahead so that the need to emulate Lot's wife is avoided.

Most of this walk lies within or along the boundary of an artillery range. At weekends there is usually no artillery practice, but phone 01–450 9845 (Mon–Fri 10.00–17.00) for information.

Car only. Take the N81 for about 17.7km/11miles south of Blessington turning left at The Olde Tollhouse for Donard. In Donard take the road east towards the youth hostel (this is straight ahead but the offset crossroads in Donard may cause brief mystification). Shortly after passing the hostel turn right and follow the road to Knockanarrigan crossroads. Turn left here and drive 2km/1.2miles to Fentons Pub at Seskin. The trek from here to Lugnaquilla passes through military lands and walkers should not stray off the route.

Walk back a few metres beyond the pub and up the road behind Fentons to the T-junction at the base of Camarahill. This road, on which private vehicular traffic is not allowed, is in a very poor state of repair with crater-like pot-holes. Continue straight ahead through a gate to follow a way-marked track, which soon peters out to become an intermittent path. This is the start of the climb to Lugnaquilla.

On this ascent Camarahill (*Caméirí*, Curving Hill, 480m) is followed by a slight dip, otherwise it is a continuous uphill all the way to the summit of Lugnaquilla. But be not faint-hearted: magnificent views unfold as you ascend, while ahead the huge block of Lugnaquilla beckons, the focus of the day's walk. The last part of this ascent is through a rock-strewn, steeply rising area. Keep left here to view the great cliffs of the North Prison.

The summit of Lug is described in Walk 23. For navigational purposes we need only note here that the top is a virtual plateau of short grass topped by a mighty cairn.

The descent is tricky in mist and, at least initially, requires careful navigation to avoid the cliffs of the North and South Prisons. Descend very gradually northeast for about 300m before turning northwest to follow the high ground downwards for about 2km to the col facing Camenabologue. Take care on this descent to avoid the long west-running spur of Cannow and two rounded mounds of high ground to the east of the route. As already said this is a marvellous stretch with a lovely panorama of peaks, prominent among which is the great whale-backed ridge of Tonelagee. Watch out along here for Art's Lough tucked in below the cliffs north of Clohernagh. Watch out even more to avoid two spurs heading northeast of the correct route which would terminate in grief and painful backtracking above Glenmalure.

The descent over firm ground comes to a sticky end in the peat hags and soggy ground south of Camenabologue (*Ceim na mbulog*, Pass of the Bullocks,

758m) and is followed by a sharp pull-up to its summit, crowned by a large reassuring cairn — reassuring because its magnitude is unique in this area.

Descending north from Camenabologue the next landmark is between it and Table Mountain where an ancient track from Glenmalure crosses west into Imaal. Turn left (west) here and almost immediately take the left fork downhill, following a track, until a forest and metal gate are reached after 2km. Here an Army way-mark, reinforced by a stern Army notice, directs the cowed traveller right downhill, forest on the left. Cross two footbridges further down and pick up a forest track beyond them. (Note that recent felling means that the maps give an impression of much more forest than actually exists.) Follow this track until you come to a forest entrance with a gate and stile and a track heading diagonally away southwest. Cross the stile and a short pleasant walk brings you to a tarmac road where you will notice another road directly opposite. Follow this road southwest for about 2km back to Fentons and perhaps some well-earned refreshments.

Distance: 18.5km/11.5miles. Ascent: 850m/2,800ft. Walking time: 6¾ hours.

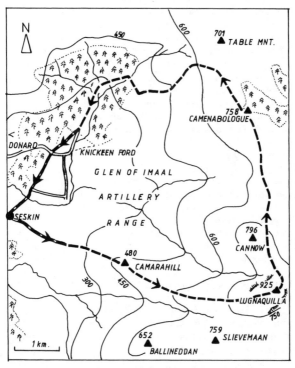

Reference OS Map: Sheet 56 (1:50,000).

28. CHURCH MOUNTAIN AND LOBAWN

*From the mountains of the western fringe the eye is inevitably drawn
towards the lush plains of Kildare and beyond. The scenery close at
hand is generally uninspiring though Lobawn towards the end of the route gives
fine views over the wide, almost mountain-enclosed basin of the Glen of Imaal.
Mostly firm underfoot conditions, interspersed with some very soggy stretches,
make for generally easy progress.*

By car take the N81 about 17.7km/11miles south of Blessington and
turn left at The Olde Tollhouse. Park in Donard (932 976). The walk may
also be adapted to suit those staying at Ballinclea Youth Hostel.

From the village walk north on tarmac, cross Hell Kettle Bridge and
take the first right turn beyond. Walk between high hedges which all too
effectively block the view, and continue beyond the last farmhouse (about
1.5km up) for approx. a further kilometre. Take the track to the left at the
first junction to follow the new forestry perimeter fence in a dogleg to the
summit of Church Mountain. Worth noting is the 'Caution Bull' sign at the
farmhouse as there sometimes is a bull.

Church Mountain, 544m, is crowned by a truly enormous heap of
stones, for which there seems to be no logical explanation. Of yore the local
speculation was that it was building material for St Kevin's road which ran
into Glendalough, a bizarre suggestion given its lofty and inconvenient
location. This might be a suitable subject for conjecture as you head to the
pass to the southeast over heather, deep drainage ditches and recent
planting which make the going hard. Pick up a bog road towards
Corriebracks, 531m. This road fails to muster enough enthusiasm to climb
to the summit and no wonder, for it must be the most unimposing soggy
pudding bowl of a mound in the entire Wicklow Mountains.

After Corriebracks descend south over a broad ridge, forest close on the
right and further away on the left and then climb to the crest of the spur
extending west from Lobawn, guided part of the way by a fence on the
right. At the crest, where views over Imaal and beyond to bulky Keadeen
are suddenly revealed, turn left (east) and following an intermittent ditch
marked by occasional stone pillars climb Lobawn (*Loban*, Little Loop,
636m). The stone pillar on the summit of Lobawn is inscribed W↑D No. 13,
the W↑D referring to 'War Department' and the pillars marking the
boundary of Army territory in the Glen of Imaal.

Descend southwest from Lobawn to the confluence of three streams at
the forest edge. Follow the perimeter fence upwards for about 30m to the
southwest. The entrance to the forest is marked by the remains of a stile and
brings you onto the end of a forest track. This track improves to a side road
after you fork right at the next junction and ends on a comparatively main
road near Snugboro Bridge. Turn right and walk the 2.5km into Donard.

Distance: 17.7km/11miles. Ascent: 700m/2,300ft. Walking time: 6¾ hours.

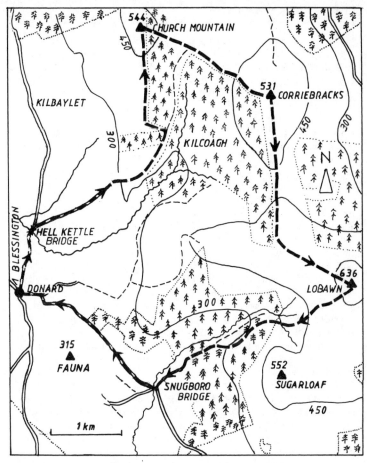

Reference OS Map: Sheet 56 (1:50,000).

29. KEADEEN

Keadeen, the most westerly of all Wicklow's mountains and thus commanding good views over the plains of Kildare and beyond, is separated from its neighbours to the east by a narrow strip of low ground. You can climb it and Carrig, its satellite to the south, or you can combine this route with route 30 to make a full day's walk.

By car take the N81 to the turn for Donard 17.7km/11miles south of Blessington. Turn left here, go through Donard to Ballinclea Youth Hostel and turn first right beyond it. Continue straight ahead for 2.6km/1.6miles and veer right with the main road to cross a bridge. Turn left immediately after it and park in the nearby car park on the left opposite the Dwyer-McAllister cottage (966 912).

Turn right out of the car park, take the first track on the left about 300m away and walk round a bend to the right to meet a forestry plantation shortly after. Follow the plantation track, curving right on it and staying with it until it ends in a turning circle. Face uphill and, with mature forest on your left and young trees on your right, follow the line of a mossy stone wall upwards between them. At the top of the forest cross the stile and walk directly ahead, due south, to the summit of Keadeen (*Céidin*, Flat-topped Hill, 653m). Its isolated position ensures excellent views. Particularly noteworthy is the great double-walled ring fort at Brusselstown Ring close below. How much more impressive it appears from here than from the Ring itself!

From Keadeen continue south following an earth-bank to the saddle facing Carrig (you can of course do a there-and-back to Carrig from here, though it offers only a minor variation in views from those seen already from the loftier Keadeen). From the saddle the aim is to head directly to the corner of forest to the northeast. Before reaching it on a direct bearing you should hit the crest of a broad spur carrying a rudimentary track. This spur gives good long views north and south (but not simultaneously).

At the corner of forest continue downhill, forest on the left and what could be a track or a firebreak underfoot. As you near the road, with fields now on the right, keep on the track (it's undoubtedly a track now) as it enters forest. The track ends at another junction and a right turn here will lead you back to the nearby road. On the road turn left to walk 2.5km to the start.

Distance 10.5km/6.5 miles. Ascent 480m/1,600ft. Walking time: 3¾ hours.

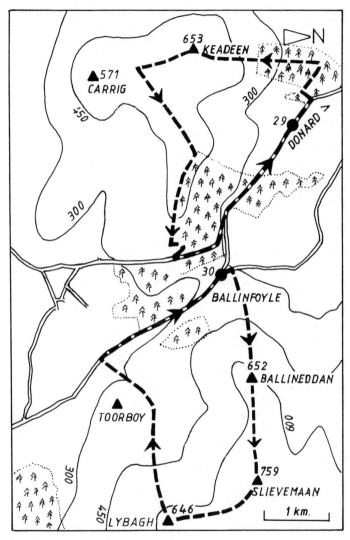

653 KEADEEN

▲571
CARRIG

450

300

300

29 DONARD ⌐

30

BALLINFOYLE

652
▲ BALLINEDDAN

600

▲
TOORBOY

759
▲
SLIEVEMAAN

300

1 km.

450
LYBAGH

646
▲

Reference OS Maps: Sheets 56 and 62 (1:50,000).

30. SLIEVEMAAN

Ballineddan, Slievemaan and Lybagh are three rather undistinguished outliers of Lugnaquilla itself, but combined they form a pleasant and undemanding circuit over fairly easy, unforested ground. From Slievemaan it is easily possible to extend the route to Lugnaquilla itself and so make a more demanding circuit. Alternatively (or even in addition) it is easy to combine this route with Walk 29 above.

By car take the N81 to the turn for Donard 17.7km/11miles south of Blessington. Turn left here, go through Donard to Ballinclea Youth Hostel and turn first right beyond it. Continue straight ahead for 2.6km/1.6miles and then keep on the main road to veer right over a bridge. Turn left immediately after it and fork left after 3km/1.9miles from the bridge. Park near the T-junction a little way further on (987 903).

From the T-junction, walk north about 70m to a gate on the right, cross it and walk the rough track beyond into nearby open country. From here it is an easy walk with gradually expanding views to the summit of Ballineddan (*Baile an fheadáin*, Homestead of the Streamlet, 652m), which has a tiny cairn and gives a good foretaste of the views to be had further up.

The slight drop after Ballineddan preludes a steady climb with excellent underfoot conditions to Slievemaan. On the way you will pass a large heap of rocks which, having read this, you will not mistake in bad weather for Slievemaan itself. Slievemaan (*Sliabh meadhoin*, Middle Mountain, 759m) has a boggy undistinguished summit but the views, especially towards the nearby huge mound of Lugnaquilla, are superb.

The route continues southeast for less than 1km along a broad ridge before swinging south to reach the summit of Lybagh, 646m, which is little more than a shoulder with not even a substantial cairn to distinguish it.

The descent from Lybagh follows the spur due south initially, then heads southwest across heathery country towards Toorboy Mountain. As the slope levels out a low stone wall crosses your path horizontally, so you can't miss it. Bear right downhill with the wall, keeping it on your left all the way to where it ends at a gate and the Derreen River is on your right. Go through the gate and walk southwest, with the river on your right and below you, to descend to a road near a stone bridge. Turning right walk across the bridge and follow the road uphill for 2km to the start.

Distance: 10.5km/6.5 miles. Ascent: 480m/1,600 ft. Walking time: 3¾ hours.

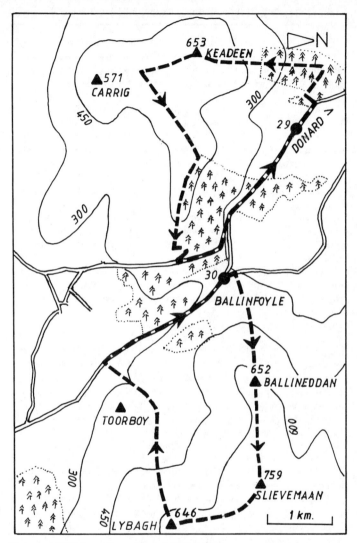

Reference OS Maps: Sheets 56 and 62 (1:50,000).

31. CIRCUIT OF THE OW VALLEY

This route, taking in Lugnaquilla and the Ow Valley to its south is a long though not very demanding walk. The wide variety of scenery is unfortunately not matched by variety of slope — nearly all climb to Lug and nearly all descent after it. At least it has the virtue of simplicity.

Car only though this walk may also be done from Aghavannagh Youth Hostel. Drive to Drumgoff crossroads as described under Walk 23. From here drive for a further 8.8km/5.5miles passing the hostel on the right and parking a little way beyond it on the right at the new bridge and entrance to the forest (055 861).

Walk about 1km west along the road to a road junction on the left (signposted Aughrim). Turn right here through an iron gate and take the track beyond and upwards towards a lonely farm overlooking the Ow Valley. Just before the farm fork left through a gate onto a minor track and continue upwards. When the track peters out walk on up over rough ground by the forest and fence on the left to Aghavannagh Mountain (580m contour on the OS map).

From here there is an intermittent track over to Lybagh, 646m, and beyond that to Slievemaan, 759m, is a steady ascent with pleasant heathery ground and gradually widening views in all directions. Particularly noteworthy is the South Prison of Lug, whose initial formidable awesomeness increases even further as you advance.

Beyond Slievemaan the great bare rectangular bulk of Lugnaquilla dominates to the northeast, reached by a direct and obvious route, first a drop through peat hags (the one and only drop on this leg), then a sustained ascent through short, usually dry grass.

The summit of Lug is described under Walk 23; suffice to say here that the views are magnificent in good visibility and well worth studying.

The next target is Corrigasleggaun, 794m, reached by a dexterous swing to the left round the precipitous periphery of the South Prison followed by a high level stroll, nearly all gently downhill. At the one junction (small cairn) take care to follow the Corrigasleggaun rather than the Clohernagh spur. A slight detour left to survey Kelly's Lough, which may be combined with a meal stop, makes a pleasant diversion.

From the cairn on Corrigasleggaun, 794m, head down to forest on a bearing of 168° and when you reach the forest turn left. Follow the fence along the edge of the trees for approx. 35 minutes to eventually arrive at a corner where a young forest appears in front of you. Cross the fence and continue for a few more minutes until you come to a cul-de-sac. Take the green track on the right which brings you down through a pleasant stretch of mature forest to a forest track. Turn left here and walk to a junction where you go right. Continue on this track to the next junction, turning left here and walk to another junction. Go right, then follow the forest track, keeping left where yet another forest track joins from the right, to reach the bridge, tarmac road and your car.

Distance: 17.7km / 11miles. Ascent: 840m / 2,760ft. Walking time: 6½ hours.

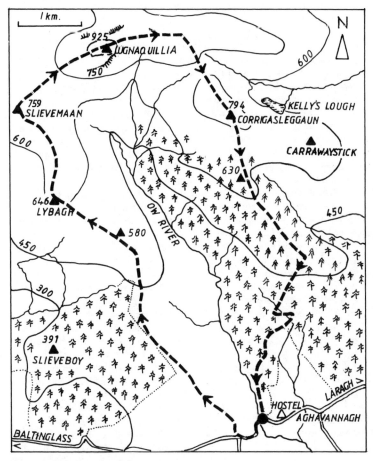

Reference OS Maps: Sheets 56 and 62 (1:50,000).

32. CROGHAN MOUNTAIN

Lying astride the borders of Counties Wicklow and Wexford, Croghan (locally Croaghan Kinsella) is a relatively distant outlier of the Wicklow Mountains. It is situated in a pleasant pastoral area with the valley of the Aughrim River to the north separating it from the bulk of the mountains. A varied scene therefore greets the walker on the way to or on the summit: pasture land and low hills near at hand, the southeast corner of the Wicklow Mountains — and indeed the Blackstairs further off to the southwest — rising beyond them.

By car drive to Aughrim on the R763 and then take the R747 (Tinahely road). 5km/3miles from Aughrim turn left (signposted 'Toberpatrick') and turn left again at the T-junction. Turn sharply first right, pass by two laneways on the left and park on waste ground on the right a few hundred metres beyond the second laneway at 105 738. (The laneway you will be walking up is this second one but it is difficult to park at the junction.)

Walk back to the laneway (106 741), walk along it and at the T-junction turn left, pass a water trough on the right and cross the gate on the right just after it. Walk diagonally upwards across the field, avoiding gorse if you can, and cross the fence at the top corner to emerge onto a grassy track. Remember this route as it will be useful on the return!

Turn left onto this track and follow it as it zigzags uphill along the northwest spur of Croghan Mountain. As you walk the view opens up to reveal a vista of rolling fields and forest, with the bulk of the Wicklow Mountains behind.

Stay with the track until it starts to contour when you pick up an old track which gradually leads to the fence on the left or head directly to the fence. Climb steeply, keeping the fence on your left, to a three-way fence junction at the top of the spur. Cross the two stiles and head east to the summit of Croghan Mountain (*Cruachain*, Hill, 606m), crowned by a formidable outcrop of rock and a tiny trig. pillar.

Head directly east to forest, keeping a fence on the left and noting the excess of stiles hereabouts — would that some of them could be moved further on to where there is a deficit — and at the forest turn left and keep it on the right round a corner and until the ground starts to drop ahead. Here descend steeply heading for the corner of another block of forest to the north.

At the corner of this forest you will have to decide whether to push on to Ballinasilloge. It is marginally worth the effort for the new views it offers, though the fences to be crossed on the way may be a deterrent. If you wish to climb it, simply keep the forest on the left (there is a small path inside the forest fence) and then climb to another block of mature forest which is as good an indication of the indistinct summit as any.

Back at the corner of the forest mentioned in the last paragraph walk downhill, forest on the right, and at a combined wall, earth-bank and fence (the first fence on the descent) turn left to follow it over rough country, crossing a stream on the way. Very soon after the stream head downhill on a grassy path as far as a wall and walk left along the grassy track parallel to the wall. On it you will cross another stream, which issues from an embryonic corrie cut into the north of Croghan.

Still on the track, climb the spur ahead, crossing a fence back into forestry and a young plantation. Take care not to step on the trees some of which have been planted on the track. At the top of the spur you will find that this is the grassy track you left near the start of the walk. Cross the fence again (now on the right) and retrace your route to the start.

Distance: 13.7km/8.5miles. Ascent: 610m/2,000ft. Walking time: 5 hours.

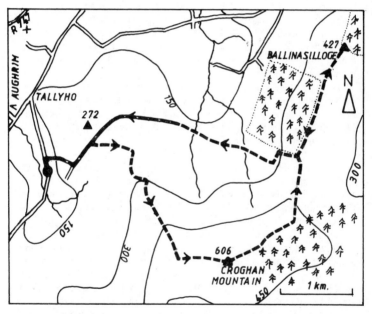

Reference OS Map: Sheet 62 (1:50,000).

33. BLACKSTAIRS MOUNTAIN

The 'tail' of the Blackstairs from its southern tip to the Scullogue Gap is just one ridge wide. This ridge falls gradually to east and west into the rich pastures of Wexford and Carlow. The walk described here covers the northern end of the 'tail', that is the central section of the entire range, taking in the granite tors around Caher Roe's Den and Blackstairs Mountain itself. It ends with a pleasant stroll through country lanes.

Drive to Ballymurphy, a village situated 5.5km/3.5miles west of the Scullogue Gap on the R702. From here take the road signposted St Mullins and Glynn, turn left off it after 1.3km/0.8mile and continue straight on for about another 2km/1.2miles to where the road swings sharply right (792 451).

Park just beyond the bend. On the left, before the farm, a gate opens onto open land. Up on the hillside you can see a green road slanting up to the right (south) to the saddle between Carrigalachan, 463m, and the main mass of Blackstairs Mountain. Go through the gate (you can actually see some remains of green road a few metres inside) and walk diagonally up the hill, passing successive walled corners of pastures to the green road, which is followed to the saddle.

At the saddle turn northeast onto the main ridge to climb the rock-strewn shoulder, marked by a massive tor. Descend the small drop beyond and then resume the upward and fairly steep climb to Blackstairs Mountain, a climb enlivened by the spectacle of the rocky teeth of granite protruding from its western flank (one of these is Caher Roe's Den).

The summit of Blackstairs Mountain, 735m, is a slight disappointment: a small cairn set on a flat area of scattered peat hags. Beyond it Mount Leinster, topped by its TV transmitter, dominates the view ahead with Knockroe a nearer and lower rounded peak across Scullogue Gap. From the summit continue more or less north (it is important not to bear too far to west or east) along the broad ridge until the road from the Scullogue Gap to Ballymurphy comes in sight. Aim 2–300m to the left (west) of the woods, cross a vague track running diagonally down to the west, and you will find a grassy track between high stone walls barring your way. At the east end where it turns downhill there is a gate. This track has become very overgrown so it is better to hop into one of the adjoining fields and head straight down to the road, rather than to try to follow the track down.

On the road turn left and walk west along it for about 2.5km to the crest of a low hill. The road swings sharply left here and as it resumes its original direction, take a left turn onto a narrow road. This road, in parts scarcely more than a lane, runs in a meandering course between high hedges and stone walls and in its course passes through the tiny hamlet of Walshstown nestling in a pronounced dip in otherwise undulating terrain. Directions along here need be minimal only: continue straight ahead to the T-junction and turn left here within a few hundred metres of the car.

Distance: 13km/8miles. Ascent: 640m/2,100ft. Walking time: 5 hours.

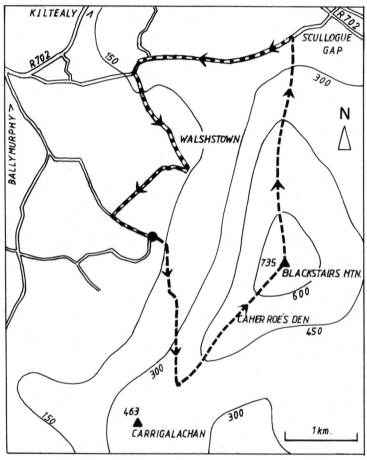

Reference OS Map: Sheet 68 (1:50,000).

34. MOUNT LEINSTER FROM THE SOUTH

From Scullogue Gap this walk takes in the broad ridge of bare, heathery mountain to its north. The route is an unbroken climb to Mount Leinster except for the substantial drop north of rounded Knockroe. It culminates in Mount Leinster itself, at 795m the highest peak in the Blackstairs. The return is over its southwest spur, descending beyond it along the deeply incised valley of a minor tributary of the River Barrow.

Take the R702 to the one and only crossroads (not signposted) at the top of the rather indeterminate Scullogue Gap. Turn north here (i.e. right from the Kiltealy direction), and turn left at the T-junction a short distance on, thus taking a side road to the north of and roughly parallel to the R702. From this T-junction drive about 1.5km/1mile to the crest of the hill (806 492) and park near a convenient laneway or rough fields on the right to avoid crossing enclosed fields.

Walk diagonally right steeply uphill towards Knockroe, 540m, through rough, pathless, rocky terrain aiming, as you advance, for the cross which, you may be heartened to learn, is very close to the top. Knockroe has a well-built cairn (plenty of raw material lying about), the outline of a house and even a rain gauge for good measure (both senses).

Heading north of Knockroe descend to the broad saddle between it and Mount Leinster, upland fields on the right, and cross a track coming up from Scullogue Gap. Continue up through high heather to the southern spur of Mount Leinster, descend slightly beyond the spur and then climb through boulders to the summit plateau.

Mount Leinster stands at the centre of four distinct spurs and, as is appropriate to its height, commands good views over most of the Blackstairs, the south of the Wicklow Mountains, including pre-eminently Lugnaquilla, and a wide variety of low hill and agricultural country. Its attraction is, of course, severely diminished by the sore thumb of the TV transmitter though the associated buildings blend in quite well with their surroundings.

Boulders and steep ground slow progress initially on the descent southwest towards Crannagh Mountain, which is but a slight rise, the huge array of boulders hereabouts being a clearer distinguishing mark. From Crannagh aim southeast for the junction of Mountain River, the main stream flowing from under the summit of Mount Leinster, with the tributary that rises in the gap north of Knockroe. That way you can be sure of keeping clear of the forestry until you pick up a track near the stream which winds through the young forest and down to the road near Rathanna. Turn left here and left again at the fork to reach the car.

Distance: 10km/6.3miles. Ascent: 760m/2,500ft. Walking time: 4½ hours.

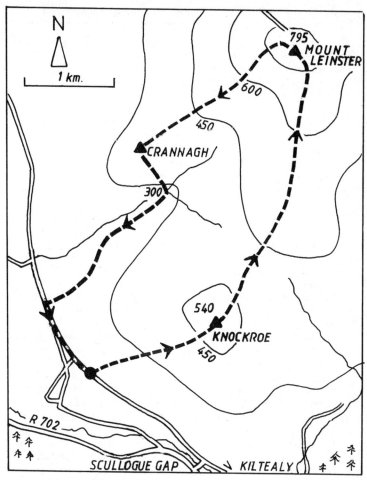

N

1 km.

795
MOUNT
LEINSTER

600

450

CRANNAGH

300

540

KNOCKROE

450

R 702

SCULLOGUE GAP   KILTEALY

Reference OS Map: Sheet 68 (1:50,000).

35. MOUNT LEINSTER AND BALLYCRYSTAL

The major exception to the general north–south trend of the Blackstairs is provided by the undulating spur reaching out east to Black Rock Mountain. This is probably the most interesting approach to Mount Leinster; the spur makes for a varied and scenic walk, and after the slog south beyond it, the remote basin of Ballycrystal forms a leisurely end to an easy day.

When you have found the start of this walk, relax — most of your navigational problems are behind! From the village of Kiltealy take the R702 towards Enniscorthy, branching left onto the R746 towards Bunclody after just over 1.5km/1mile. Turn left at the multiple junction 2.6km/1.6miles further on and left again a few hundred yards on. Drive straight on for 2.6km/1.6miles and park at a forest entrance on the right just before a bungalow at about 852 512.

Walk past the bungalow and the narrow strip of mature forest beyond it and turn right through a gate between the forest and a field. Walk to the top of the forest, pass through another gate and continue directly upwards to the crest of the ridge, picking up a useful track (but useful for a short time only) near the crest. The large flat-roofed, stone building at the crest is worth inspecting. The summit of Black Rock lies a few hundred yards further east and is a there-and-back which may be visited by purists or those who do not intend to tell even little fibs about the mountains they climbed.

The rest of us will head directly west to Mount Leinster, climbing on the way a couple of rocky protuberances. An area of strewn boulders beyond them marks the upper slopes of Mount Leinster.

From the summit, described under Walk 34, head south along the spur ending in Knockroe keeping to the east side (of the spur). Here you may recoup the cost of this book by betting (but not too insistently, mind) that the track to which you are heading is not rising, though to the naked eye it certainly appears as if it is.

Take this track (and it is level!) to the south and then southeast and when it disappears collect your winnings and head down to the ruin with the two beautiful beech trees at the southwest corner of Ballycrystal (at this point the track has re-emerged and can be seen sneaking round to the ruin).

Take this track north (it shortly graduates to a narrow road) which a little way down passes through a region of pleasant forest. From here it is but a short walk through mixed farmland and forest back to the car.

Distance: 10km/6miles. Ascent: 580m/1,900ft. Walking time: 4 hours.

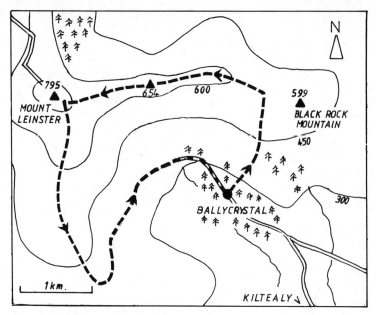

Reference OS Map: Sheet 68 (1:50,000).

SOUTHEAST AND MIDLANDS   Miriam Joyce McCarthy

INTRODUCTION

This guide is basically a series of route descriptions intended to help people find their way on and off the hills. It should be helpful to those new to hill-walking or experienced walkers to this area. Of course, there are many routes and endless variations of those described.

The routes described range from short rambles along tracks to longer trips for experienced walkers with navigational skills.

The following walks are totally on tracks and enable one to experience a mountain environment without the associated risks:

Walks 36, 37, 43, 45 (B), 63 (B) and 65, have tracks leading all the way to the summits.

Walk 41 has a path and Walk 59 has a track leading to two spectacular corrie lakes. Walks 52 and 53 combine to make up the East Munster Way, a low-level, way-marked trail.

Walks 54, 55 and 56: the first sections of these walks have tracks going well into the mountains to elevations of over 600m. All other routes are on open moorlands and should only be attempted by walkers with mountaineering skills.

It is advisable to walk the routes in the direction in which they are described to avoid any difficulties of access.

Hill-walkers in the southeast have always enjoyed a special relationship with the local farming communities and this should be maintained by following the Farmland Code of Conduct given at the beginning of this book.

In wishing you enjoyable and memorable walking, may I protect myself by saying that although in the preparation of this guide I have been as careful as possible, I take no responsibility for the reader's failure to travel in safety.

I wish to thank the many people who helped me in the completion of the guide. The members of the Peaks Mountaineering Club who walked with me and stood patiently while I took notes — James Bond, Ann Butler, Trish Butler, Breda Costigan, Mary Lonergan, Ellen O'Donnell, Jim O'Neill. I am grateful to Pat Holland for advice on the antiquities of the area. Many thanks to Tom Joyce who contributed the walks in the Slieve Blooms; to Niall Carroll and the late Tony O'Brien for their local knowledge and advice on the Comeraghs; to Sr Brendan Keating and Cait Ni Mhaolachtnaigh for material on local history. Thanks to Greg Kenny for his tape recorder and to Joss Lynam for his help during the preparation of the book.

I'm particularly grateful to Justin McCarthy for the benefit of his mountaineering experience and his extensive knowledge of the Galtees; for walking with me every Sunday and for his help, encouragement and understanding when the pressure was on.

ACCESS AND ACCOMMODATION

The mountains of the southeast of Ireland are very accessible both to the Irish hill-walker and the visitor from abroad. There are passenger/car ferry services from Britain to Dun Laoghaire (Dublin) and Rosslare daily. Continental visitors can take the ferry direct to Rosslare from Le Havre or Cherbourg and be in the mountains within a few hours of arrival in the country. There are airports at Dublin, Cork and Waterford.

The area is well served by major roads. The N8 from Dublin to Cork runs through the region, and the Cahir to Mitchelstown section is parallel with the southern slopes of the Galty Ridge. The N8 also passes within a few kilometres of the Slieve Bloom at Portlaoise. The N24 from Limerick to Waterford passes close to the Galtees, Comeraghs and Slievenamon. The Silvermines and the Keeper Hill area can be approached from the N7 Dublin to Limerick route. The Knockmealdowns are within 20km of the N8 and N24 at Cahir, and are divided by one of the finest mountain passes in the country — the Vee on the R668 between Clogheen and Lismore.

The main railway line from Dublin to Cork also runs through the region, the most imposing sight during the journey being the superb backdrop of the Galtees as the train pulls in to the busy station of Limerick Junction. Express buses run between the major towns but there is no public transport into the mountains.

Information on travel and accommodation can be obtained from the Southeast Tourism, whose head office is at 41 The Quay, Waterford, Tel. 051-75823. This office operates throughout the year but most towns have tourist information offices open to visitors during the summer months.

The southeast region is well endowed with accommodation of all types from Grade A hotels to country homes, hostels and caravans and camping parks.

The following is a small selection of places where mountaineers are especially welcome.

Town and Country Homes
 (i) Hanora's Cottage, Nire Valley, Co. Waterford. 052-36134.
 (ii) Mrs Ryan, Clonanav Farm House, Nire Valley, Co. Waterford. 052-36141.
(iii) Homeleigh Farm House, Ballynacourty, Co. Tipperary. 062-56228.
(iv) Ballyglass House, Glen of Aherlow, Co. Tipperary. 062-52104.

Hostels

An Oige

  (i) Ballydavid Wood, Youth Hostel, Glen of Aherlow, Bansha, Co. Tipperary. Open 1 March–30 November. 062-54148.

  (ii) Mountain Lodge, Youth Hostel, Burncourt, Cahir, Co. Tipperary. Open 1 April– 30 September. 052-67277.

  (iii) Lismore Hostel, Lismore, Co. Waterford. Open 1 April–30 September. 058-54390.

Private Hostels

  (i) Farmhouse Hostel, Cahir, Co. Tipperary. 052-41906.

  (ii) Lisakyle, Cahir, Co. Tipperary. Open all year. 052-41963.

  (iii) Powers The Pot, Harney's Cross, south of Clonmel, Co. Tipperary. 052-23085. The owner is an experienced mountaineer and his advice should be both appreciated and heeded. Open 1 March–23 December.

Caravan and Camping Parks

  (i) The Apple, on the N24 between Cahir and Clonmel. 052-41459.

  (ii) Ballynacourty House, Glen of Aherlow. 062-56230.

  (iii) Powers The Pot, Harney's Cross, south of Clonmel. 052-23085.

There are mountaineering clubs in Clonmel, Kilkenny and Waterford. Their members walk these mountains regularly and the addresses and telephone numbers of the current secretaries can be obtained from the Mountaineering Council of Ireland, c/o AFAS, House of Sport, Longmile Road, Dublin 12. Tel. 01-450 9845, Fax 01-450 2805.

GEOLOGY

Were it not for the mountains and valleys we would not be able to enjoy this exhilarating recreation. A little knowledge of what shaped the landscape will help one to appreciate its natural beauty and grandeur. The study of the shaping processes is a highly complex and vast subject. In dealing with it I will attempt to be as simple and straightforward as possible.

The highlands of the southeast of Ireland were formed about 300 million years ago in the Devonian period when adjustments in the earth's crust caused tremendous lateral pressuring to occur. These pressures forced the crust to crumble into folds. Subsequent erosion of the higher folds has in general caused the mountains as we know them. The extent of the erosion, however, is dependent on the hardness of the rock at the top of the fold so that in some cases the upward folds correspond with ridges of high relief and in others they have been worn down completely to form valleys and lowlands.

The high mountains of Waterford composed of old red sandstone (ORS) overlook the coastal plains and the beautiful valley of the Blackwater River.

In the west the complex upfold corresponds with the Knockmealdown mountains to the east; the Comeragh and Monavullagh mountains are also composed of ORS, where hundreds of metres of purple grits and brownish conglomerates and shales have been upfolded into a gigantic arch. The eastern end of the arch has been worn down to reveal a rolling plateau of Silurian rocks, known as the plateau of Rathgormack — a fertile tract of farmland in contrast to the heathery hills of sandstone.

The Galtees, lying 32km/20miles north/northwest of the Comeraghs form a high ridge, in contrast to the plateau of the latter group. Rising abruptly from the plain of Tipperary with high grassy peaks and deep gullies, the Galtees form a very imposing group. Devonian folding has caused the ORS to protrude through its covering of carboniferous limestone and silurian rocks to protrude in their turn through the ORS, so the striking characteristic of the Tipperary landscape is the way in which the landforms alternate between the slate and sandstone of the hills and the limestone which largely composes the valleys and plains. The famous Mitchelstown Caves owe their origin to the soluble properties of carboniferous limestone.

The streams which drain the corries of the Galtees flow steeply down the northern slopes into the picturesque Glen of Aherlow, once famed for its forest cover but now occupied by prosperous farmland on the limestone soil. The woodlands are now of the coniferous variety and are state plantations. The wooded Slievenamuck ridge forms the northern side of the glen.

Like the plateau of Rathgormack the anticlinal arch of Slievenamon has been breached on its eastern side to uncover Silurian grits and slates, where the ORS rises to 722m. The Devil's Bit mountain, the Silvermines and Keeper Hill in north Tipperary were also formed by folding in the Devonian period and are composed of sedimentary rocks similar to the mountains further south.

The ridge of the Slieve Bloom in Laois/Offaly contains the most northerly anticlines of the Armorican foldings in the southern half of Ireland. The carboniferous limestone has since been worn down to expose the underlying sandstone and slates. The highest point of this range is Arderin, 528m, which, like all mountains of the Devonian period, has been lowered drastically by weathering and erosion in the 300 million years since being formed.

The direction of the folding in Munster is generally east–west and is termed the Armorican trend because it can be traced in the rocks of Armorica (Brittany). The north–east, south–west trend of the Caledonian period of mountain buildings (associated with the northern half of the country) can be seen in the north–south axis of the Comeraghs.

But it was the action of glaciers during the Ice Ages which carved the most spectacular features of the Irish mountains and which gives them their greatest appeal. (They began 1 million years ago and lasted until 10,000 years ago.)

The Galtees, Knockmealdowns and Comeraghs were too high to be over-ridden by the inland icesheets but they had their own local glaciers. The higher peaks protruded above the icesheets as nunataks and were subjected to the constant severe frost shattering, causing the rocks to fissure into grotesquely shaped outcrops. Particularly good examples are O'Loughnan's Castle, west of Greenane on the Galty Ridge and the summit of the Galtymore itself.

The eastern and northern faces of the Comeraghs have been extensively gouged out by a series of local glaciers leaving behind several superb corries, precipitous cliffs, glaciated valleys, hanging valleys and waterfalls. The gigantic amphitheatre of Coumshingaun is one of the finest examples of a corrie in these islands and has a back wall which rises 500m vertically above the lake, exposing a considerable part of the old red sandstone layers. The valley southwest of the gap is a hanging valley though not as spectacular as the Eagles Nest in the Magillycuddy Reeks; while the glaciated valley of Coumiarthar contains a series of small rock-basin lakes in hollows deepened by glacier which once occupied it.

The material excavated by the ice was deposited on the valley slopes as moraine and now often acts as a dam trapping a lake behind it. Good examples are to be found in the Galtees and Comeraghs.

After the glacial period, Ireland experienced a mild wet climate and forest and peat bogs became extensive. Only a small amount of natural oak forest remains — near Cahir — but the mountains contain vast areas of heather-clad blanket bogs.

FLORA AND FAUNA

FLORA: With the exception of a few notable areas where a combination of particular conditions have provided a rich habitat — Mount Brandon in Co. Kerry is a good example — there is on Irish mountains a relative scarcity of species which in Britain, for instance, are more common. This certainly applies in the southeast where hills are covered by a blanket of species of poor acid grassland having as its main components common bent grass (*Agrostis tenuis*), wavy hair grass (*Deschampsia flexuosa*), sheep's fescue (*Festuca ovina*), sorrel (*Rumex acetosa*), sheep's sorrel (*R. acetosella*), heath bedstraw (*Galium saxatile*), bell heather (*Erica cinerea*), deer grass (*Scirpus cespitosus*) and ribbed sedge (*Carex binervis*). Sundew (*Drosera*), an insectivorous plant, can be found in wet flushes.

However it has been claimed that botanical surveys of Irish mountain regions derive a peculiar zest from the very poverty of flora in alpine species (Nathaniel Colgan in *The Irish Naturalist*, 1900) and if this is accepted the corries of both the Galtees and the Comeraghs have much to excite the botanist. The former in particular provide interesting outlying stations for St Patrick's cabbage (*Saxifraga spathularis*) — one of the Lusitanian species of the Irish flora and a relative of the urban London Pride — the mossy saxifrages (*S. rosacea* and *S. hypnoides*) and mountain sorrel (*Oxyria digyna*). St Patrick's cabbage, which has an otherwise limited distribution in southwest Europe, has its main stations in south and west Ireland and in the Galtees is reported from Loughs Muskry and Borheen.

The mossy saxifrages occur at all the Galty corries as do green spleenwort (*Asplenium viride*) and cowberry (*Vaccinium vitis idaea*), whilst mountain sorrel and dwarf willow (*Salix herbacea*) are missing only from Lough Borheen which is the least alpine in character. Other species of interest growing mainly by Loughs Curra and Muskry, but also beneath the bluffs on the northern side of the Carrignabinnia/Lyracappul ridge, are brittle bladder fern (*Cystopteris fragilis*), rose root (*Rhodiola rosea*), filmy fern (*Hymenophyllum wilsonii*) and scurvy grass (*Cochlearia officinalis*). Strangely alpine saw-wort (*Saussurea alpina*) is reported as occurring only at the rather gloomy Lough Diheen though here limited botanical exploration of the range could be the reason.

In the Comeraghs the same factors of Silurian shale cliffs facing generally away from the sun and the lack of grazing combine to make the corries the most interesting ground for the botanist. Coumshingaun is the main centre, for St Patrick's cabbage, mossy saxifrage (*hypnoides* but not *rosacea*), rose root, Welsh poppy (*Meconopsis cambrica*) and marsh hawksbeard (*Crepis paludosa*) all occur there, and St Patrick's cabbage also grows close to Crotty's Lake and Coumduala.

Due to the relative absence of suitable cliffs the Knockmealdowns are much poorer botanically than the Galtees and Comeraghs, though the broken ground north of the main summit again yields St Patrick's cabbage and mossy saxifrage (*S. hypnoides*). Further west the great banks of rhododendrons (*R. ponticum*) rising almost vertically behind Bay Lough are a familiar sight to thousands of travellers, for the Vee Gap road runs along the opposite side of the valley.

The hills of north Tipperary are also of little interest to the botanist, the only notable plant of the area being cowberry on Keeper Hill. Hay-scented buckler fern (*Dryopteris aemula*) and mountain fern (*Thelypteris limbosperma*) also occur both here and on the Silvermines ridge, and the lesser twayblade orchid (*Listera cordata*) is the other species growing on both sides of the Mulkeir valley.

One of the most attractive spots in the Slieve Bloom is just north of Arderin, where valleys from each side of the range meet to form the Glendine Gap. It is also the most botanically rewarding spot in the range for Welsh poppy and the two ferns mentioned above are found close by. The peat bog which covers these hills is otherwise uninteresting, and the same can be said of Slievenamon which has only stiff sedge (*Carex bigelowii*) growing on the stony ground close to the summit.

Personally I have a great liking for the late summer flowering rowan tree (or mountain ash, *Sorbus aucuparia*) which grows by most of the valley streams in the region, though less frequently in the Comeraghs. I must admit also to less affection for whortleberries (*Vaccinium myrtillus*) which are plentiful almost everywhere, and which until a few years ago were picked and exported to South Wales as an energy food for miners. Driving around the lanes close to the Monavullaghs will be made all the more pleasant by the presence of fuchsia (*F. magellanica*) which though not as verdant here as in the west is just as welcome.

The lower slope of all the ranges are heavily forested. There is unquestionably a certain monotony in passing through these almost totally coniferous plantations but from the hilltops they add variety to the otherwise regular pattern of fields. Sitka spruce, imported from north America because of its remarkable growth record in poor soil, is the most common tree in these forests, often accompanied by Douglas fir, Scots pine, Norwegian spruce and larch. Sadly there are relatively few deciduous trees, though traces of the great forests which once completely covered the area can still be seen in the Glen of Aherlow. Scaragh Wood near Cahir has patches of natural oak and its associated ground flora.

FAUNA: The fauna of Ireland are not nearly as well documented as the flora, particularly when one attempts to relate it to a particular geographic feature such as mountains. There are, however, certain species of birds and animals which are known to be present generally and these, augmented by some personal sightings, form the basis for the notes which follow.

On the moorlands, and particularly on the less desolate hillsides, one invariably meets the ubiquitous skylark (*Alauda arvensis*), whilst yellow-hammers (*Emberiza citrinells*), meadow pipits (*Anthus pratensis*), pied wagtails (*Motacilla alba*), stonechats (*Saxicola torquata*) and the occasional grey wagtail (*M. cinerea*) also tend to favour this type of terrain. Another attractive bird often seen in bracken or rushes is the hen harrier (*Circus cyaneus*) which breeds around the edge of forestry plantations and has a predilection for red sandstone areas. Game such as grouse (*Lagopus lagopus*) and pheasants (*Phasianus colchicus*) prefer blanket bog and sparse heather — the former are particularly numerous in the Slieve Bloom — and damp moorland is also favoured by curlews (*Numenius arquata*) which are now much less common than a few years ago. Short turf such as that grazed by sheep attracts wheatears (*Oenanthe oenanthe*), whilst scree slopes and crags are the habitat of ravens (*Corvus corax*), jackdaws (*Corvus monedula*) and the rare kestrels (*Falco tinnunculus*) and peregrine falcons (*Falco peregrinus*). Other birds of prey which frequent the region are merlins (*Falco columbarius*) and, generally at lower levels, sparrowhawks (*Accipiter nisus*). When walking by the mountain streams you may also have the pleasure of seeing the fascinating dippers (*Cinclus cinclus*) — there is an Irish subspecies — which are present throughout the region though I have observed them only in the Comeraghs. This may be due to their early nesting, in February or March, and the early breeding of the ring ouzel (*Turdus torquatus*) may also account for the lack of recent information on this now relatively rare visitor.

I should also record that there is a chance of seeing herons (*Ardea cinerea*) in the mountains too. Mention should be made of the hooded or grey carrion crows (*Corvus corone cornix*) which are present in large numbers on all the lower slopes.

The only reptile in Ireland is the common or viviparous lizard (*Lacerta vivapara*) whilst insectivores are represented by hedgehogs (*Erinaceus europaeus*) and pygmy shrews (*Sorex minutus*) though there is little information as to the height at which these may be encountered. There is a very interesting concentration of wood ants (*Formica lugubris*) in the forests on both sides of the Galtees, and though there are a few nests in the woods of the northern Knockmealdowns, they are extremely rare elsewhere in Ireland. It is now considered possible that they were introduced into the dense woods of Tipperary as a food for pheasants.

The mammals include the nocturnal — and thus rarely seen — badger (*Meles meles*) and the far-ranging red fox (*Vulpes vulpes*) which can be spotted regularly up to the highest reaches of all the southeastern mountains. Fallow deer (*Dama dama*) occur in the woods on the slopes of the Galtees, Knockmealdowns and Comeraghs. The best time of the day to see them is at dawn or dusk. There is, however, a large herd of feral goats (*Capra*) on Slievenamuck and there are also goats — large in size if not in number — on the Knockmealdowns. Mountain hares (*Lepus timidus hibernicus*) are commonly seen at height on all the hills whilst in the limestone valley rabbits (*Oryctolagus cuniculus*) show many signs of recovery from the myxomatosis virus of the 1950s. And as you make your way through the forests you may be fortunate enough to see the delightful red squirrel (*Sciurus vulgaris leucourus*) or less likely the unobtrusive pine marten (*Martes martes*). Other mammals which should be mentioned are woodmice (*Apodemus sylvaticus*), which are found on many mountains, and brown rats (*Rattus norvegicus*) which are now unfortunately so numerous as to require very thorough control.

Fishing stories relating to mountains seem to be no less embellished than those elsewhere and I have often heard of gigantic trout (*Salmo trutta fario*) being taken from the Galty and Comeragh lakes. The fish are certainly there but, in my experience, gigantic they most definitely are not! There is also an interesting old record of char (*Salvelinus alpinus*), a fish belonging to colder climates but left in isolated localities since the glacial period, emanating from the Coumalocha on the western edge of the Comeraghs.

Given reasonable conditions butterflies can often be found on the highest summits, so although recording applies in the main to lower levels there is a reasonable guide to the possibility of finding certain species when hill-walking. The speckled wood (*Pararge aegeria*), wall brown (*Pararge megera*), meadow brown (*Maniola jurtina*), small heath (*Coenonympha pamphilus*), ringlet (*Aphantopus hyperanthus*), small tortoiseshell (*Aglais urticae*), and large, small and green-veined white (*Pieris brassicae, rapae* and *napi*) are common almost everywhere, whilst the hedgebrown (*Maniola tithonus*) and dark green fritillary (*Argynnis aglaia*) are more likely to be seen around the Monavullaghs. The specialist may also be able to spot the grayling (*Eumenis semele*), common blue (*Polyommatus icarus*), small copper (*Lycaena phlaeas*), green hairstreak (*Callophrys rubi*) or marsh fritillary (*Euphydryas aurinia*) though the latter is rather rare even on the boggy areas which are its habitat.

Finally please remember that all of nature's works are seen to best advantage in their own setting and should therefore not be disturbed or interfered with in any manner whatsoever.

ANTIQUITIES

The story of man's involvement with the southeast of Ireland and its mountains seems to have begun about 4000 B.C. when the first farmers came to the country. Few traces of their settlement have survived though a good number of their tools, such as polished stone axeheads, are known.

The stone tombs in which they buried their dead remain, however. There is a passage tomb at Slievenamuck overlooking the Glen of Aherlow from the north and perhaps also under hilltop cairns such as those at Temple Hill, Slievenamon and Knockshanahullion.

Monuments of the succeeding Bronze Age (*c.* 2500–300 B.C.) in which man began the use of metal, include stone tombs and there are several wedge tombs and a stone circle in the Silvermines. Standing stones like that associated with a burial site at the Barnamadra gap or close to the Nire Valley car park may date from the Bronze Age.

Settlements of the Iron Age, the period traditionally associated with the Celts, may include some of the many ring forts visible from the mountains.

Later in the fifth century A.D. we begin to enter the region of written history with the introduction of Christianity. The mountain routeway known as Rian Bo Phadraig which leads over the Knockmealdowns is supposed to have linked Cashel with Lismore. Routeways such as this may be of greater age and could even date back to prehistoric times. They were used up until comparatively recent times, before the advent of motorised transport.

Traces of the recent past, such as potato ridges indicating the terrible pressure for arable land in the last century, can be seen on the slopes of the Galtees.

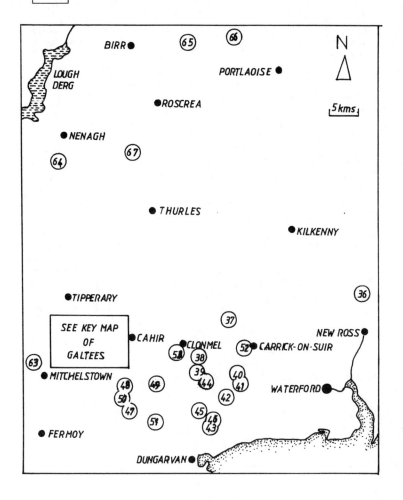

36. BRANDON HILL

On the west side of the River Barrow the clear-cut cone of Brandon Hill rises from the river bank to 515m. It forms part of the southern edge of the granitic mass of the Leinster Chain. The wooded slopes of Brandon give an added charm to the little town of Graiguenamanagh nestling by the river at its foot. Its summit is a fine viewpoint and it is an ideal hill on which to take the family along for a stroll.

Take the Inistioge road out of Graiguenamanagh and after 3.9km/2.4miles you will come to a lane on your left with a derelict house at the entrance (1.1km/0.7mile before the bridge). Drive up this lane, which is rough in spots, to a forestry barricade, 1.3km/0.8mile, where there is parking for three or four cars.

Walk up along a forestry road to where it forks. Take the left option and continue along this ascending road around the head of the valley, until it emerges out on the open moorland. There are lovely views of Graiguenamanagh beneath you through the mature forest.

When you emerge from the forest, bear right along the forest edge for 150m. Then turn left uphill along a wide spur following a worn track for 120m towards the large steel cross (erected by the people of Graiguenamanagh). The summit cairn of Brandon Hill, 515m, is just behind the cross.

The views from here are superb, the River Barrow meandering peacefully beneath you, the Wicklow and Blackstairs ranges to the northeast and east. On a clear day you can see as far as Waterford Harbour and Hook Head.

Descend by retracing your steps or by following the track which descends from the summit along the western edge of the forest to where you join the forest road again.

Distance: 6.4km/4miles. Ascent: 300m/980ft. Walking time: 2–2½ hours.

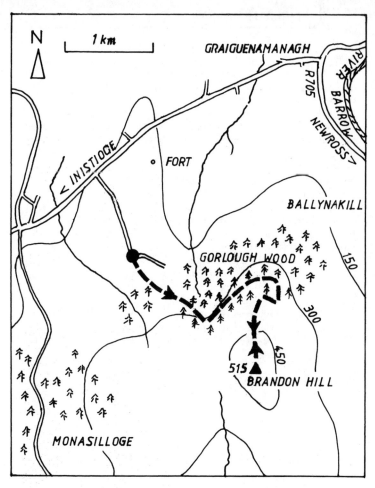

Reference OS Map: Sheet 68 (1:50,000).

37. SLIEVENAMON

(Sliabh na mBan, *Mountain of the Women of Fionn*)

According to legend, the large cairn on the summit of this great sandstone cone is where Fionn Mac Cumhaill sat waiting for Grainne, daughter of the High King, Cormac Mac Airt. They were in love and wished to marry but Fionn was so popular with the ladies, the King decided that there would be a race up these slopes and whoever reached the top first would win his hand. Fionn showed Grainne a short cut up the mountain and she was victorious.

The ascent from Kilcash (314 280) is very straightforward and requires no navigational skills as the route is entirely on a track.

To get to the starting point take the N24 and N76 from Clonmel. After about 13km/8miles turn left towards the village of Ballypatrick, at which you turn right for Kilcash. Drive through Kilcash and turn left at the top of the hill. About 0.5km/0.3mile past a sharp right-hand bend there is a farmyard. Park here (317 288).

Take the lane on the left-hand side of the road. Follow this lane through a gate and out onto the open mountain. Here, bear right and follow a new track with a wood on your right. Continue on this track up to the summit cairn, 721m.

Near the summit you will come across an unsightly building which bears testimony to local needs for multi-channel television.

Retracing your steps offers an excellent opportunity to enjoy the unique vista of the Suir Valley.

Distance: 5km/3miles. Ascent: 480m/1,600ft. Walking time: 2½ hours.

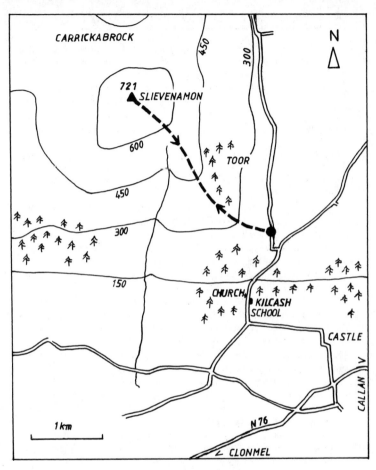

Reference OS Maps: Sheets 67 and 75 (1:50,000).

38. LONG HILL AND LAGHTNAFRANKEE

The northern foothills of the Comeraghs fall directly towards the valley of the Suir and the town of Clonmel. It is a very accessible and popular walking area among the local inhabitants.

There are traces of old routes marked on the map and discernible on the ground — linking Clonmel with the villages of Glenary, Glendalough and the Nire Valley. The walk I have chosen to describe takes in Long Hill, the Glenary River and Laghtnafrankee.

Take the R678 east from Clonmel and after about 5km / 3miles, just past the entrance to the golf club, park near Laurel Bridge by a gate leading into the forest on your right (238 196).

Walk directly along the forest road towards the head of the valley to emerge into the punchbowl, a large natural amphitheatre. Turn right along the outside of the forest. Then, shortly, bear left and walk up to the top of the ridge using a small cairn as your target. As you walk, generally northwestwards, towards Long Hill, 404m, you will see the lush farmland of the Suir Valley and the town of Clonmel with its expanding suburbs just beneath you to the north. Along here also you will see low pillars marking a former firing range.

Descend 100m to a col. A few hundred metres to the northwest is a large cross and altar erected in 1956 by the people of the Old Bridge area of Clonmel. You may wish to detour to it. (One can descend directly to Clonmel from the cross.)

Return to the col and then southwest to the ruins of what must have been a beautifully situated farm. This is an ideal spot to take a break.

Proceed southwards towards the Glenary River by staying right of a forestry plantation going downhill. Cross the river by the stepping stones. Just west of here is the old deserted village of Glenary — today a lonely forgotten place which may be tedious to reach from this side.

Keep the forest on your right as you begin to go uphill again. When you get above the trees you will arrive at the first of two cairns from which you must turn east along the top of another broad ridge. Running at right angles to your route is the dramatic northern Comeragh ridge culminating in Knockanaffrin, while below you to the south are the picturesque woods of the Nire Valley and the village of Glendalough. After passing the 425m point, bear left slightly downhill to a minor col crossing an old route known as the Staire. This old route, discernible in places on the ground, connected the Nire with Clonmel. Then 120m of uphill will take you to the triangulation point and cairns at the summit of Laghtnafrankee, 520m.

The direct route back to your car is to head due north down into the punchbowl and the forest.

Distance: 10km/6miles. Ascent: 600m/1,950ft. Walking time: 4 hours.

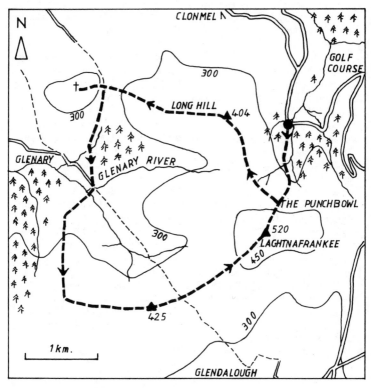

Reference OS Map: Sheet 75 (1:50,000).

39. KNOCKANAFFRIN RIDGE

This ridge is known locally as the 'Seven Sisters' because of its rocky outcrops when viewed from the eastern side. Though there are limited opportunities for easy scrambling it is a fine, invigorating but easy walk.

The starting point I prefer is at Glenanore (261 145) which enables you to enjoy this lovely ridge walk and be able to return to your car without having to retrace your steps.

From Ballymacarbry (on the R671 south of Clonmel) take the road which goes eastwards along the southern bank of the River Nire (Nier) to the Nire Church. Just beyond the church turn left and go straight to the end of the road and the village of Glenanore (not named on OS map), where there is parking for just a few cars. This village was far more densely populated in years gone by, judging by the number of deserted houses there now.

A rough track leads towards the mountains from the village. As you set off you will catch glimpses of the ridge through the trees. Cross the stream and head uphill in a northeast direction over grassy slopes towards Knocksheegowna, 678m. As you pause for a breather you might see traditional turf cutting in progress below you in spring and early summer. Laghtnafrankee can be seen to the northwest and the Knockmealdowns and Galtees in the distance.

Knocksheegowna (Hill of the Fairy Calves) is soon encountered and is a good place to take a rest and absorb the beauty of your surroundings. The lovely name of this peak is derived from a legend about the lake below to the left, Lough Mohra, reputed to be the home of a herd of milk-white cows tended by a beautiful water sprite.

This ridge makes for easy navigation and the direction is generally south.

The northeast slopes are steep, boulder-strewn and wooded, with pleasant views of the corrie lakes below, the first of which soon becomes visible — Lough Mohra (*Loch Mor*, ironically one of the smallest in the Comeraghs) in the shadow of Knockanaffrin.

Knockanaffrin, 755m, is the highest point along the ridge. Translated, it means Hill of the Mass — one of two places bearing that name in the Comeraghs, the other being a townland in the Nire Valley. In penal times Irish people often had to resort to an isolated townland or a lonely mountain peak to attend Mass in peace.

The peak itself is a jumble of fractured conglomerate rock with an insignificant cairn on top. Below to the southeast is the second lake-filled corrie, Coumduala (Hollow of the Black Cliff).

Descending from the top you will soon be skirting the dangerous cliffs over Coumduala along a well-worn path which leads down to the Gap.

From here on a sunny winter's day the coums of the Comeraghs present a very impressive picture — from Crotty's Rock in the east to the Sgilloge lakes in the west.

The Gap itself had an old route running through it — which can still be discerned — from the Nire Valley to Rathgormack.

Return to Glenanore by the lower western slopes of the ridge. Pass across the spur which descends from Knockanaffrin and head towards the stream you crossed at the start of the walk. Pick up the track and return to Glenanore.

Distance: 11.3km/7miles. Ascent: 580m/1,900ft. Walking time: 4 hours.

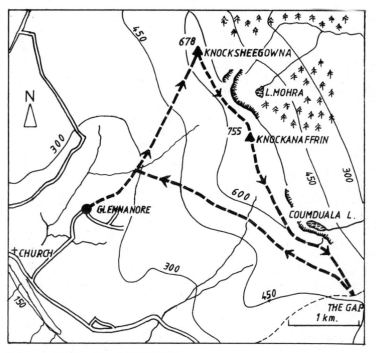

Reference OS Map: Sheet 75 (1:50,000).

40. CROTTY'S LAKE AND ROCK

William Crotty, a highwayman, was the leader of a gang of outlaws in the eighteenth century who used the Comeraghs as their base. Even the OS has agreed to accept the name for the lake and the outstanding pinnacle above it. He harassed the countryside from the Comeraghs to the coast. He robbed the rich and gave to the poor and accumulated a considerable treasure for himself. The mountainside was his refuge — in a cave beside the lake. It was known only to his wife and himself and could only be entered by way of a 'chimney climb'.

His look-out point was an outstanding pinnacle on the northeast edge of the Comeraghs just above the lake itself — now called Crotty's Rock. From here he could easily spot soldiers toiling up the slopes, in plenty of time to make his escape.

Crotty was finally captured, tried and hanged in Waterford in 1742 on information supplied by David Norris — one of his faithful band of followers — who betrayed him. Afterwards Norris, afraid of revenge and perhaps hoping to lay his hands on some of Crotty's hidden treasures, persuaded the authorities to put a price on the outlaw's widow. After being pursued by soldiers, she killed herself by jumping to her death from Crotty's Rock.

Crotty's lake, the scene of these tragic happenings, is one of the most beautiful and peaceful places in the Comeraghs and is easily accessible. The lake itself is a fine one with towering cliffs rising above it though not as high as those at Coumshingaun.

From Ballyhest crossroads (368 154) on the R676 (Carrick-on-Suir to Dungarvan road), take the second road on the right. After about 0.8km/0.5mile there is a rough lay-by on the right opposite double farm gates (348 136). Park here.

Walk up the road for another 800m to a farmhouse on the left. Having sought permission here proceed along a well graded track behind the house. Follow it upwards until it runs out, after which you will be on rough moraine until you reach the lake (20 minutes). It is advisable to follow a wire fence on your right until you get to a ramp with an obvious boulder on the near skyline. A small dry ravine leads quickly to the northwest corner of the lake.

The edge of the lake is a perfect place to rest a while and absorb the beauty of the coum and the spectacular buttress.

Crotty's Rock
To get to this feature, walk along the moraine at the front of the lake to its southeast corner. The large 'rock' above you is Crotty's Rock. You can walk up along a heathery slope and emerge on top beside large boulders at the base of the rock.

The most interesting route (though tedious at first) in my opinion is to follow a sheep track and broken fence in the direction of a short gully with a pillar on its right.

Pass below this pillar and ascend a broad, steep, easy gully which will take you to Crotty's Rock without too much difficulty. On emerging from the gully turn left to the large outcrop of conglomerate rock which is Crotty's. Take note of the low arch in the outcrop. The story goes that after going through this arch the first person you meet will be your life's partner!

You are now on the desolate Comeragh plateau. Proceed in a westerly direction to the top of a steep, glaciated valley which contains a group of small, beautiful and lonely lakes, which are simply Coum Iarthar Loughs on the OS map. The largest of them is Coumgorra, the Lake of the Echoes. A tributary of the Clodiagh River flows out of these lakes. You can descend close to them by taking the eastern spur.

Eventually you will have to contour back to Crotty's Lake — the western edge, where you will be able to enjoy once more the solitude of this splendid coum. From here your steps take you back to civilisation.

Distance: 8km/5miles. Ascent: 640m/2,100ft. Walking time: 3½ hours.

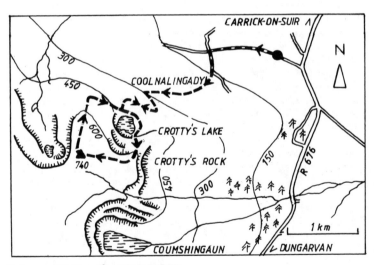

Reference OS Map: Sheet 75 (1:50,000).

41. THE CIRCUIT OF COUMSHINGAUN

The gigantic glacial amphitheatre of Coumshingaun (Hollow of the Ants) is claimed to be the finest example of a corrie in these islands. Situated very close to the main road, it is a perfect place to experience a mountain environment with very little effort.

The lake itself, the largest in the Comeraghs, is said to be 'bottomless and containing evil spirits'! Less than one hour's walk from the road, it is a popular location for family picnics. The towering cliffs rising above the lake have many rock-climbing routes, most of which get infrequent ascents.

The route around the encircling coum is perhaps the finest and most invigorating walk in the Comeragh Mountains. The southern ridge offers some enjoyable but easy scrambling, the nearest thing to the Kerry Reeks in this part of the country.

The starting point (349 116) is close to a bridge on the R676 about 14.5km/9miles south of Carrick-on-Suir. The bridge is over the stream which flows down from the lake. Park close to the junction of a minor road.

Enter by a gate across the main road and follow the track down to the stream and across a grassy field and some scrub. (The area inside the gate tends to be very muddy in winter. In these circumstances, the alternative route is through a large field just south of the gate.)

Cross the stile out onto the open mountain and follow a clear path in the direction of the corrie. This path continues underneath the end of the north shoulder and on to the lake. From the lake take the southern spur which becomes an arête. As you move along, doing some mild scrambling, you will be rewarded by spectacular and plunging views down both sides — glimpses of the lake beneath you to your right as you move around the rocks and views into a deep narrow valley on the opposite side.

These rocks lead to a grassy section with a sheep track to the left of the crest. The last scramble up to the plateau must be taken with great care and is not at all suitable for inexperienced walkers. Once on the plateau you will be able — on a clear day — to see the Waterford and Wexford coastlines.

You may wish to detour towards Fauscoum, 792m, the small cairn which represents the highest point in the Comeraghs. Fauscoum rises only a few metres above the surrounding boggy plateau and may be difficult to locate.

Back to the cliff edge again — head around the rim of the corrie toward the grassy cone of Stookanmeen (Smooth Peak, 704m). Proceed along the northern spur keeping the stream Iske Sullas (Water of Light) on your left.

Descend carefully over rough terrain, taking care not to leave the spur too early and end up on steep ground over the lake.

When you finally reach the vicinity of the lake you deserve a rest and an opportunity to admire the splendour of Coumshingaun, and retrace with your eyes the route you have just taken. You must eventually drag yourself away from the serenity of this place and head back to the hustle and bustle of civilisation.

Distance: 8km/5miles. Ascent: 700m/2,300ft. Walking time: 4 hours.

To the lake and back
Distance: 4km/2.5miles. Ascent: 240m/800ft. Walking time: 1¾ hours.

If you wish to gain direct access on to the southern spur and arête, park your car in the car park in Kilclooney Wood (341 103) 1.5km further south along the R676.

Follow a short well-worn path through the wood until it joins a forest road. Take a right turn along the road until it runs out. Cross a fence and follow a stone wall up along the spur.

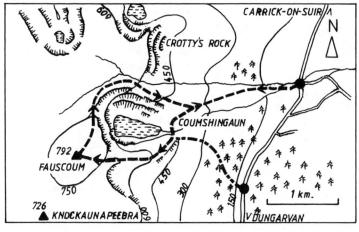

Reference OS Map: Sheet 75 (1:50,000).

42. THE MAHON FALLS AND COUMTAY

The upper section of the Mahon River is a rugged and beautiful place, one of the finest in the Comeragh Mountains. This broad, glaciated valley has a large stream, the sources of which rise in the desolate plateau above, before converging and tumbling down in a series of spectacular cascades with precipitous walls. In summer it forms rock pools with just a trickle of water flowing over the boulders but in winter it falls in a really impressive drop of around 150m.

It can be reached by turning west off the R676 (north of Dungarvan) at Mahon Bridge (Furraleigh, 343 060). Turn right immediately by a shop following the signs for 'Comeragh Drive'. In a little over 1.5km/1mile turn right along a road with the Mahon River on your right. Park in the car park where the road turns south at 314 078.

Two large boulders mark the footpath which leads directly to the bottom of the falls. Cross the stream over the stepping stones where the footpath meets the stream. (N.B. It is sometimes impassable in wet winter conditions and climbing to the left of the falls is not advisable.) Climb steeply along faint tracks with the falls on your left.

Cross the river above the falls and head uphill in a south-westerly direction over a wide plateau with the infant Mahon tributaries draining down from the marshes and peat hags. The area, however, offers some of the finest views in the southeast. The majestic cone of Knockaunapeebra, 726m is behind you, while southwards you have fine views of the Waterford coastline and Dungarvan Bay — if the day is good! You can also see Seefin, 726m, the highest point of the Monavullaghs with its ugly building spoiling this wilderness area.

Further along the route you will approach the narrow neck where the cliffs of Coumfea to the north and Coumtay to the south are only a few hundred metres apart. On your way you will catch glimpses of Slievenamon, Knockanaffrin and, in the distance, the Galtees and Knockmealdowns.

Turn in the direction of Coumtay. Circle around the edge of the cliffs and only begin to lose height when you reach the far end of the southern encircling spur. When you drop down to the end of the spur turn left and cross the valley by the ruins of an isolated house.

Walk uphill along the forest edge and back along the road to rejoin your car.

Distance: 10.5km/6.5miles. Ascent: 400m/1,300ft. Walking time: 4 hours.

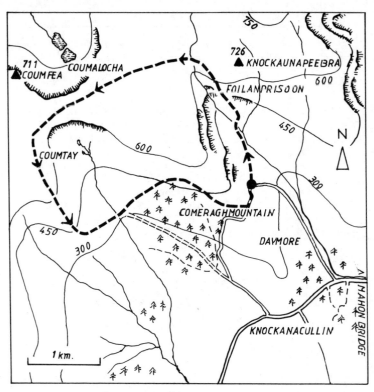

Reference OS Map: Sheet 75 (1:50,000).

43. CROHAUN

*The little cone of Crohaun, 484m, stands alone just south of the main
Comeragh range. It is separated from Farbreaga by a broad col. A very
scenic road runs through it (from Lemybrien to Kilbrien) which rises to around
339m at its highest point.*

From Dungarvan take the N25 to Lemybrien. Follow the signs for
'Comeragh Drive' on roads heading west or northwest. Cross Dalligan
bridge and park at the top of the road (271 016) a few hundred metres
beyond a large lay-by.

A track leads south from the road along the forest edge to a TV mast.
Continue up the ridge to the summit cairn.

The views from here are superb — Dungarvan town, the Bay of Helvick
Head to the south; the sandy beaches and cliffs from Tramore round to
Youghal seem almost beneath your feet. The Comeragh Mountains stretch
northwards through the heart of County Waterford.

Distance: 2.4km/1.5miles. Ascent: 150m/500ft. Walking time: 1 hour.

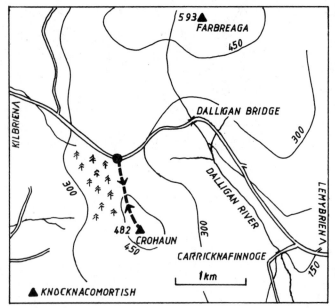

Reference OS Map: Sheet 75 (1:50,000).

44. CIRCUIT OF THE NIRE VALLEY

The word Comeragh comes from 'Cumarach' which means full of hollows, glacial in origin. Indeed the majority of Comeragh names incorporate coum (hollow or valley) in some form. The main tributary of the Nire (Nier) rises from the most easterly of them — the Sgilloge Loughs and is joined by other streams. The Nire itself rises from the central group, the Coumalochas, and to the west is one more, the highest, the deepest and the largest, Coumfea.

From Clonmel take the R671 south to Ballymacarbry. Drive eastwards along the valley of the Nire River towards the Nire church. Pass the church and carry on to the large lay-by above the river (276 129). The lay-by is a very popular place in summer. It overlooks the Nire Valley and is an ideal spot from which to explore these mountains.

From your starting point you can see clearly (on a fine day) the outline of your day's walk — Coumfea the westernmost coum, the Coumalochas, the Sgilloge Loughs and Coumlara, all north-facing coums and all except the last one containing attractive little lakes.

From the car park walk down the road for 500m to a gate on the left. Follow a track down to the river observing a number of small sheltered green fields around Lyre. Cross on a wooden bridge (which you may notice has not been grant-aided by the EU structural funds!).

N.B. This river is prone to flash floods and the water level may rise well above the bridge after a spell of heavy rain.

Continue along the track which will join an old track coming from Lyre. Cross over to this track by the stepping stones. Go up the track to a gate and out onto the open mountain where you veer right towards a fence. Follow the fence which leads roughly southeastwards in the direction of the western shoulder of Coumfea.

You will be rewarded by spectacular views of the coums on your left with their sheer precipices dropping down to the lakes which are the special splendour of the Comeraghs.

Having reached the spur the route continues uphill in a southeast direction along a gentle grassy slope. The cliffs of Coumfea are just below you on the left. A tiny cairn marks the summit of Coumfea, 711m.

You are now on the relatively featureless plateau of the Comeraghs, which in these parts offers some pleasant walking and fine views — the lakes nearly 300m below, the Gap, the Knockanaffrin ridge, the valleys of Nire and Lyre and, in the distance, other mountains.

Soon, you will be just above the coum containing the Sgilloge Loughs, beside a little stream which plunges steeply over rocks to the inner lake below. The northwest winds blow the spray back upwards along cliffs (known as *Sean Bhean ag caitheamh tobac*, Old Woman Smoking a Pipe)

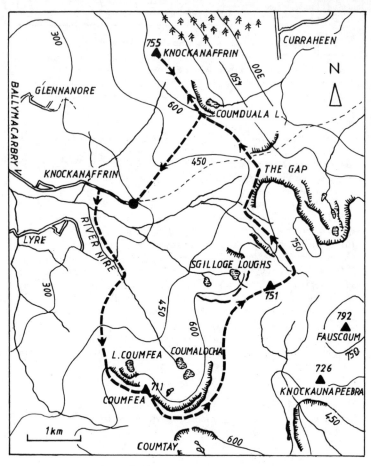

Reference OS Map: Sheet 75 (1:50,000).

which in winter freezes into weirdly shaped icicles on the vegetation and rocks.

About 500m of uphill walking will take you to 751m and the head of Coumlara. This valley is narrow and, on its western side, steep. It contains a sparkling stream which runs busily down the first few hundred metres and then meanders gently as the valley floor levels out towards the Gap.

Descend by the middle of the valley over ferns and mosses, keeping the river on your left. Alternatively, if you are fortunate enough you will pick up a contouring sheep track on the eastern slope which will take you all the way to the Gap.

At the Gap you now have a choice — of continuing the circuit by taking in Knockanaffrin or returning directly to the lay-by. If you decide on the latter, follow the white stakes out to the lay-by in order to avoid the marshy ground lower down.

If you decide on taking in Knockanaffrin you can look forward to enjoying some very pleasant, easy walking up along the ridge. You will be surprised how quickly you will gain height.

After approx. 45 minutes and about 300m of ascent you will be on top at 755m.

Descend by retracing your steps to the cliffs above Lough Coumduala. From here walk in a southwest direction along the spur which drops down directly to the lay-by.

Distance: 17.7km/11miles. Ascent: 820m/2,700ft. Walking time: 6½ hours.

45. SEEFIN AND FARBREAGA HORSESHOE

The Monavullagh Mountains, of which Seefin is the highest point, are a continuation of and very similar to the Comeraghs. The name 'Monavullagh' itself means 'Turf at the top of a hill'. In fact the valleys are much drier and the tops far less boggy than the Comeraghs.

The circuit of the Araglin valley is a very pleasant walk with many spectacular views of mountain and coastline and is an easy route from a navigational point of view.

Approx. 14.5km/9miles northwest of Dungarvan on the R672 you will come to a crossroads with a filling station on your left. Take a right turn for Kilbrien. After 2.9km/1.8miles you will come to Scart Bridge (Sawmills). Cross the bridge and after about 30m turn right. Immediately before Kilbrien village you will see a school on your left. Turn left after the school and travel 1.8km/1.1miles along this road to another road on your left. Take this road for 2km/1.2miles approx., to a sharp left turn. Continue on, crossing a spur and you will find a gateway on your right with ample parking (254 048).

Begin, by walking uphill along the forest track to where it meets the main track leading to the summit of Seefin. The first thing you notice is the ugly man-made structure built for the purpose of providing multi-channel TV for places along the Waterford coast.

The summit of Seefin provides some of the finest and most extensive views of the Waterford coastline, including Dungarvan Bay and Helvick Head; the Comeragh plateau to the north and the Galtees and Knockmealdowns in the distance.

Descend southwards for about 220m along a wire fence to the Barnamadra gap (Dog's gap) in the heart of the Monavullaghs. Here there are to be seen a standing stone and a stone circle of prehistoric origin in the middle of the col.

The legendary St Declan's path went from Kilbrien and the Araglin valley through Barnamadra to Mahon Bridge and Kilmacthomas on the eastern side.

The fence continues up the opposite hillside to 617m from where the necessary direction is almost due south and then east of south across the marshy plateau to Farbreaga, 593m.

Descend by retracing your steps to the col or, alternatively, contour along the grassy slopes of the Monavullagh Mountains.

From the col make for the ruins of an old farm building with a rusty roof among a small V-shaped cluster of coniferous trees. Cross the stream, then pass through a gate where you will pick up the track which completes the horseshoe.

Distance: 11.3km/7miles. Ascent: 610m/2,000ft. Walking time: 4½ hours.

B. Alternative route

Seefin Mountain itself is a peak which is reached almost entirely on tracks so it can be enjoyed by people without navigational skills, if after reaching the peak they descend by retracing their steps.

Distance: 7.2km/4.5miles. Ascent: 460m/1,500ft. Walking time: 3 hours.

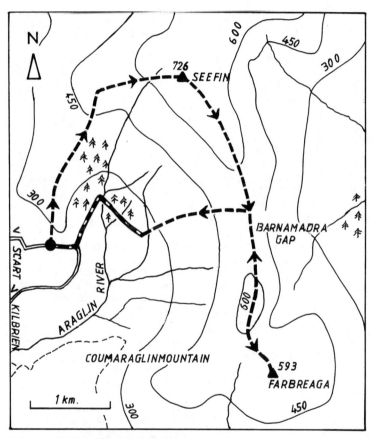

Reference OS Map: Sheet 75 (1:50,000).

46. THE FRED CAREW MEMORIAL WALK

This long-distance walk, organised by the Peaks Mountaineering Club, is held every year in April. It starts at a road junction (307 023) near the village of Kilrossanty, but access to the mountain is tricky except on that particular day. To avoid these difficulties I suggest you begin at the top of the road (271 016) southwest of Dalligan Bridge.

The route extends northwards, taking in Farbreaga and Seefin in the Monavullaghs, the Comeragh plateau, Knockaunapeebra, the Gap, Knockanaffrin and ending in Powers the Pot (256 196).

The Comeraghs have a reputation for their bogginess but the route takes in the drier sections, which makes for pleasant walking and some fine views along the way. Fred Carew, an enthusiastic walker all his life, was the first president of the Peaks Club, and continued as president until his death in 1985.

To get to the start of the walk, head for Lemybrien, a small village where the N25 joins the R676. Roads leading west from here and sign-posted 'Comeragh Drive' will take you to the col between Crohaun and Farbreaga. There is ample parking here.

Walk northwards along a gentle spur, then eastwards towards Farbreaga itself, 593m. Continue towards the broad grassy spur of the unnamed top, 617m and descend along a wire fence to the Barnamadra Gap. There is about 200m of uphill to Seefin, 726m, fairly steep at first but levelling off towards the summit.

From Seefin the route descends along the Comeragh plateau and up an almost unnoticeable 60m to the edge of the cliffs of Coumtay. Continue across land to the broad upper course of the Mahon River where you have to drop 120m and cross the river itself before rising again to the top of the twin-cairned cone of Knockaunapeebra (Hillock of the Piper, 726m). It is worth taking a short break here to take in the fine views.

Fauscoum at 792m is the highest point in the Comeraghs but it is an insignificant summit on top of an elevated bog and can be easily missed in poor weather conditions. So, in those circumstances it is prudent to take a bearing from Knockaunapeebra to the top of the narrow valley of Coumlara. This enables the walker to cross an intricate section of the Comeragh plateau on one bearing. This route also has the advantage of avoiding the 'blackest bog' of the plateau!

Take care to enter this valley on the right-hand side and follow the right-hand side of the river as you descend towards the Gap.

From the Gap climb the Knockanaffrin ridge which offers the most pleasant walking of the entire route. Continue from 755m, the highest point, to the trig. point on top of Knocksheegowna, 678m, your final peak of the day. The finish is now in sight. It is the line of coniferous trees about 4km to the northwest. From Knocksheegowna walkers who keep to the following suggestions will be rewarded by the driest line available. Descend northwest along the spur, keeping well above the river until you are in line with the buildings of Powers the Pot. Then, veer directly west, cross the stream and walk through a green field to the finish.

N.B. It is important to be aware that there is a substantial road journey between the start and the finish of this long-distance walk.

Distance: 25km / 15.5miles. Ascent: 850m / 2,800ft Walking time: 7–9 hours.

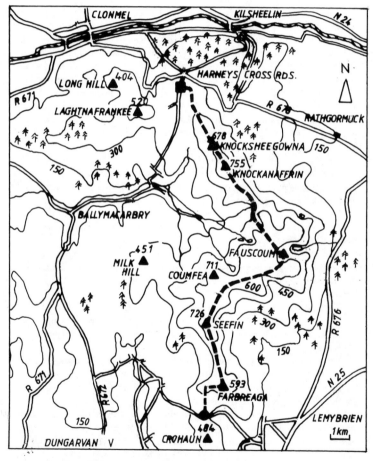

Reference OS Map: Sheet 75 (1:50,000).

47. KNOCKMEALDOWN–SUGARLOAF HORSESHOE

The Clogheen–Lismore road, R668, is one of the most scenic drives in the southeast. From Clogheen the road winds up through steep woods as far as the Vee Gap and continues southwards across moorland with superb views. The Grubb monument is about 150m beyond the hairpin bend opposite the sign for 'Premier Drive'. This tombstone marks the grave of Samuel Grubb who had lived and owned property in the Golden Vale and wished to be buried in sight of his paradise. According to to a local tale, he gave orders to be buried on the very top of the hills but six strong bearers could go no further — he would see no better on top!

Continuing along the road you come to Bay Lough on your right. It is a corrie lake, dammed by morainic deposits. It is reputed to be bottomless and inhabited by the ghost of 'Petticoat Loose'. In summer it is surrounded by a magnificent display of rhododendrons. The old road used to go straight up the valley past the Bay Lough. It is still walkable. The Sugarloaf and Knockmealdowns are on your left.

Just before the junction with the Cappoquin road (R669) you can park your car in the car park on the right, across the road from some trees which hide a derelict house (039 078).

Proceed uphill along a gentle slope with patches of short heather until you reach the summit of *Cnoc Maol Donn* (Bare Brown Mountain, 794m).

For those walkers who do not have time to continue the route you may now retrace your steps to your car.

Lismore and Cappoquin lie at the foot of the ridge while the south coast can be made out in the distance. On very clear winter days sightings of the Kerry mountains have been reported.

It is said that this was the spot chosen for burial by Major Eeles of Lismore who wrote extensively in the eighteenth century on the use of electricity as a cure for mental illness. There are no traces of his grave, however.

Descend in a northwesterly direction over short springy heather, again along the wall to a col. Ascend the final 90m of the day to the summit of Sugarloaf, 663m, a double-cairned peak overlooking the broad plains of Tipperary.

This section from Knockmealdown to Sugarloaf is the most spectacular part of the walk. The ridge is at its narrowest and the views are superb.

From Sugarloaf descend steeply, following a low wall to the large lay-by at the highest point of the Vee Gap.

The shelter at the top of the road marks the spot where Bianconi's tired stagecoach horses were changed after the long haul up from the valley below. At the lay-by also, there is an altar where Mass is celebrated every year.

Return to the car by walking along the road.

Knockmealdown Mountain

Distance: 5km/3miles. Ascent: 520m/1,700ft. Walking time: 2½ hours.

Horseshoe

Distance: 9.6km/6miles. Ascent: 610m/2,000ft. Walking time: 3½–4 hours.

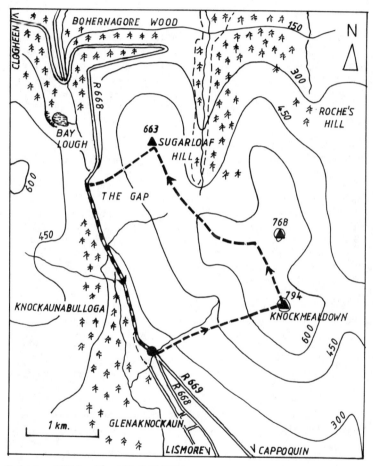

Reference OS Map: Sheet 74 (1:50,000).

48. KNOCKMEALDOWN FROM THE NORTHERN VALLEYS

This is one of the most interesting walks in this range. To gain maximum enjoyment from it, park a car at the finish, known locally as the 'Meeting of the Waters'. It is the confluence of the Glengalla River and a tributary (078 111).

The walk begins at the hairpin bend (044 118) on the way up to the Vee Gap (on the R668 south of Clogheen). There is plenty of space for parking. From this point at about 250m you can see Clogheen village beneath you to the northwest and the Comeragh Gap to the east. The Galty Mountains are slightly west of north. Castlegrace, home of the Grubb family, is in the valley slightly west of north. On a clear day you can see the Devil's Bit in the distant north.

Leave the road at the very point of the hairpin bend. Proceed northeast along various tracks dropping down towards the stream until you meet a good wide path about 50m above the stream (not marked on the map).

Follow this path south to the head of the valley where you bear left along the top edge of the wood (the tiny Lough Moylan is now dried up and surrounded by trees).

After about seven minutes there is a broad, easy gully on your right. Climb this gully southwest to the main ridge. Follow the earth ditch (at this point along the county boundary of Waterford and Tipperary) to the top of Knockmealdown, 794m.

Descend steeply east over easy ground towards a wide col. From the east side of the col follow a faint track east of north leading to a corner of a new wood (within eight minutes). Contour along the eastern edge of the wood for about 400m. Take a rough track straight down to the left. Just before you reach a small stream veer sharply right through a small opening in the trees leading to a soggy track (keeping the main stream on your left).

Continue along this track which curves round the spur until you pick up a rough road running north on the east bank of the main stream.

This area has several contouring forest roads and the important thing is to reach the rough road on the east bank of the Glengalla River at the Meeting of the Waters. If you haven't a second car, walk north along the road for 1km until you reach the East Munster Way, which you follow back west to your starting point.

Distance: 11.3km/7miles. Ascent: 550m/1,800ft. Walking time: 4 hours.

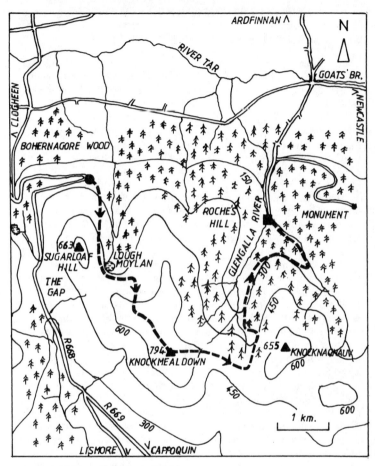

Reference OS Map: Sheet 74 (1:50,000).

49. THE EASTERN KNOCKMEALDOWNS

(From the Liam Lynch Monument to the Vee Gap)

This traverse over easy terrain takes in most of the major peaks of the range and is an exhilarating walk. The ridge forms part of the boundary between Counties Tipperary and Waterford and contrasts dramatically with the lush farms of the lowlands.

Drive to Goat's Bridge (*Goatenbridge,* 087 136) on the Clogheen to Newcastle road and turn south along a narrow road signposted to the Liam Lynch Monument. This road leads onto a forest road with several junctions all of which have signposts to the monument. Park just before the entrance to the monument at 097 110.

This monument, a small round tower for which the stone was gathered off the surrounding mountains, commemorates Liam Lynch who was commanding officer of the First Southern Division of the IRA during the Civil War. He was shot down on the mountainside near Goatenbridge in April 1923 shortly before the ceasefire.

Around the monument on the lower slopes of Crohan West there is a forestry plantation. Follow a rough track — starting about 40m west of the monument — which leads uphill through the plantation. Proceed out on to open moorland towards the top of Crohan West, 521m. Pause, now and then, to absorb the fine views unfolding all around you. (Because of the rough nature of the terrain, this route is easier to ascend than descend.)

Drop down along a wall to a col and ascend gradually over grassy terrain to Knockmeal, 560m. Descend to the southwest along a wall after Knockmeal towards the corner of a new wood. Here, you veer away from the ditch and proceed upwards to the broad summit of Knocknafallia, 668m — a strenuous ascent but you will be rewarded by splendid views from the large cairn which marks the summit. Care and precision are required to find this cairn in mist as it is off the centre of the plateau.

From here you will be able to see the southern side of the ridge for the first time — the River Blackwater meandering southwards towards Youghal Bay, the large grey buildings of Mount Melleray, a Cistercian monastery on the lower slopes of Knocknafallia, and eastwards the Comeragh Mountains.

From Knocknafallia the route now crosses a col and on to the stone-strewn ridge of Knocknagnauv (*Cnoc na gCnabh,* Hill of the Bones, 655m). Here you pick up the wall again with its small summit cairns. Descend now to the col just under Knockmealdown. An ancient ecclesiastical route (St Declan's Way) from Cashel to Ardmore passed through this col, and traces of it are still discernible.

The biggest ascent of the day now awaits you — with Knockmealdown looming up ahead! It is 300m from here to the top of the highest peak in the range, Knockmealdown itself (*Cnoc maol donn*, Bare Brown Mountain, 794m). Follow the wall, which goes steeply to the top where you will be rewarded by excellent views and the knowledge that your day's work is almost done.

The rest of the walk over the Sugarloaf to the Vee Gap is the same as Walk 47.

Distance: 14.5km/9miles. Ascent: 1,000m/3,300ft. Walking time: 6 hours.

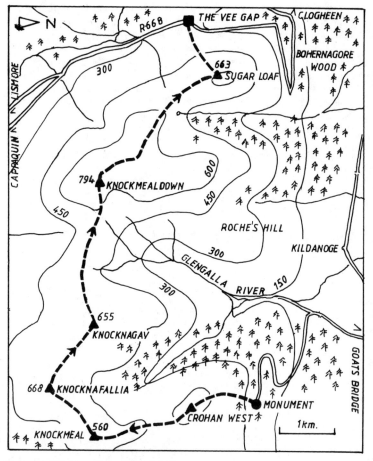

Reference OS Map: Sheet 74 (1:50,000).

50. THE WESTERN KNOCKMEALDOWNS

This route, together with the eastern Knockmealdowns, can be linked to make up a full traverse of the range.

From the Vee Gap (031 100) at the highest point on the R668 between Clogheen and Lismore, walk uphill to an unnamed peak at 630m. A faint path through the heather makes this steep ascent a little easier. As you gain height be sure to pause and take in the spectacular views all around.

From 630m drop 60m southwestwards over easy terrain to a long col. Then head in a northwest direction and up 90m to the large and impressive cairn of Knockshanahullion (Hill of the Old Elbow, 652m).

From Knockshanahullion descend south and then southwest along a broad spur to a minor road which goes through the col just under Farbreaga. This hill, 518m, is just 90m above the col. From Farbreaga head in a northwesterly direction to a rough track just west of the main stream. Follow it through a gate and onto a surfaced road and Kilcaroon Bridge (952 130). You can reduce the amount of road walking by parking your car 2km/1.2miles further in the valley from this bridge.

Distance: 12km/7.5miles. Ascent: 460m/1,500ft. Walking time: 4 hours.

An alternative which is useful if you have only one car is to return to the col from Farbreaga and follow the Avondhu Way back along the southern slopes of Knockshanahullion to the Vee.

Distance: 16km/10miles. Ascent: 570m/1,850ft. Walking time: 5½ hours.

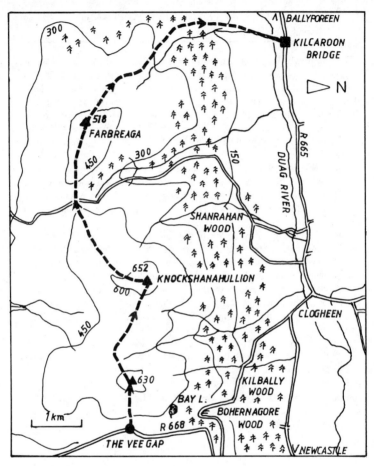

Reference OS Map: Sheet 74 (1:50,000).

51. KNOCKNAFALLIA FROM MOUNT MELLERAY

Travelling north on the R669 from Cappoquin (on the Clogheen road) take the second turning right, then left through the main gates of the monastery. At the northwest corner of the football pitch take a series of laneways running north until you reach a recently planted forest. Go along a laneway at the edge of this forest until you come to the second of two farm cottages. This spot can also be reached by driving up the road past the monastery gates (0.8km/0.5mile) and parking. Follow the laneway to the cottage.

Bear right after the cottage along a footpath which emerges onto young forest. Follow the main forest road, contouring at first and then rising gently in a direction west of north. Just after the main forest road swings in an easterly direction follow a zigzag path northwards to the edge of the woods.

Head up along a gentle spur to the summit of Knocknafallia. You will find a large cairn on the southeast corner of the summit plateau, 668m.

On the ascent there are excellent views of Mount Melleray, the River Blackwater, Knockmealdown and the Monavullaghs.

At the summit, 668m, a whole new world opens up with extensive views of all the mountain ranges in the south as well as Dungarvan Bay.

Onwards to the col under Knockmeal and a short gentle rise northeastwards, 60m, takes you to the top of Knockmeal.

Drop down in a direction south of east towards the Melleray–Newcastle road at the head of Glennafallia. From here a pleasant road walk brings you back to your car.

Distance: 12km/7.5miles. Ascent: 550m/1,800ft. Walking time: 4½ hours.

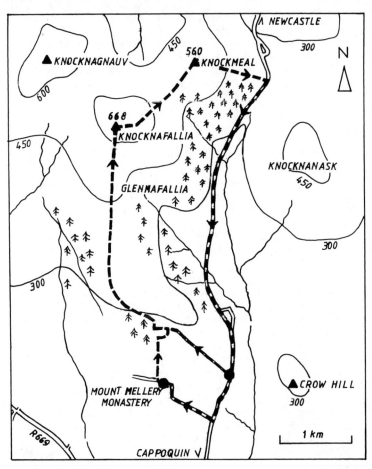

Reference OS Map: Sheet 74 (1:50,000).

The East Munster Way

The East Munster Way is a low-level, way-marked route following towpaths, old tracks, forest roads, country roads and occasionally open moorland. It is linked to the South Leinster Way and there are plans to connect it with the Kerry Way. It begins in Carrick-on-Suir and heads mainly west across south Tipperary and north Waterford to Clogheen. Strong walkers can easily reach Clogheen in two days, using Clonmel as an overnight stop. A new extension, the Avondhu Way, goes from Clogheen via the Vee to Fermoy.

52. THE EAST MUNSTER WAY: CARRICK-ON-SUIR TO CLONMEL

An old towpath by the River Suir is used along this tranquil stretch between the two busy towns of Carrick and Clonmel. The path was built in the late eighteenth century for the horses that pulled flat-bottomed boats laden with raw materials for the industries of Clonmel. Nowadays it is hard to imagine it was once the main highway of County Tipperary.

The starting point for the day's walk is the Suir towpath at the Quays in Carrick. There are so many things to be seen along this stretch of the river — many fine tower houses, traditional fishing cots, old boathouses, great varieties of wild flowers and wild life. There are, constantly, great splashes and sounds on the river itself, the moorhen, the duck and the leaping trout disturbing the calm waters.

The route leads directly along the towpath to the bridge in the picturesque village of Kilsheelan, a perfect place to pause for a while and quench your thirst.

Thus rested, cross Kilsheelan bridge and enter Gurteen wood by the old Alms House, now a private residence. The climbing track follows forest roads out of the Suir Valley with the eminence of Slievenamon framing the distant view across the rich fertile valley below. Further on there are splendid views of the Knockanaffrin ridge, the Comeragh corries in the distance and, to the west and a little closer, Laghtnafrankee and Long Hill.

The route joins a public road at Harney's Cross and from here you drop down to rejoin the towpath at Sir Thomas Bridge for the short stretch to Clonmel ending near Lady Blessington's Bath.

N.B. The East Munster Way is not marked on the current edition of Sheet 75.

Distance: 30.5km/19miles. Ascent: 310m/1,000ft. Walking time: 7–9 hours.

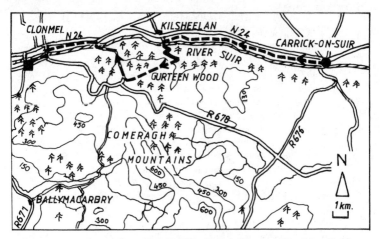

Reference: (i) OS Map: Sheet 75 (1:50,000); (ii) East Munster Way Map Guide (1:50,000), east/west mapping.

53. THE EAST MUNSTER WAY: CLONMEL TO CLOGHEEN

The starting point for this stage of the route is just south of the Old Bridge in Clonmel. Proceed to Roaring Spring road, where you veer left up a steep country road, from where markers lead you to the Holy Year Cross. This point is a prominent landmark above Clonmel and an excellent place to pause awhile and absorb the beauty of your surroundings.

From here the route veers westwards for a while before joining a very old road which is followed southwards. This road bypasses the old deserted village of Glenary and leads to a ford on the Glenary River (204 191), which is crossed to reach a forest trail leading up to a forest road where you turn right, crossing a concrete bridge. Then, turn left at two junctions, still climbing to swing away to the southwest corner of Russellstown state forest (178 168).

The Way turns left from Russellstown Forest, then forks right, down a boreen with almost as much grass as tarmac, while ahead is a splendid panorama of the Knockmealdown Mountains.

After crossing the busy R671 (Clonmel to Dungarvan road) the way winds mainly southwest leaving Four Mile Water Catholic church on the left, crossing first Four Mile Water Bridge, then Creggane Bridge, to enter County Tipperary again at 162 133.

Then the village of Newcastle is reached, and once again the banks of the River Suir, passing Bannard House on the right; from Newcastle, the Mount Melleray road is taken for some 5km. Then, look for an old track on the right, cut off from tarmac by a low stone wall (115 104). This track links with a forest road and, where a left turn leads west, passes the modern round tower monument to Liam Lynch who was killed in the Civil War 1922–3. From here the majestic outline of the Galty Mountains enhances the beauty of the surrounding landscape.

Zigzagging down, the forest road crosses a path on the site of an ancient trackway called Rian Bo Phadraig — 'The track of St Patrick's cow' — which linked Lismore to Ardfinnan and Cashel, passing over the mountains through the col just under their highest point (Knockmealdown itself).

The Way crosses the Glengalla River and continues along forest tracks, crossing the Glenmoylan River to reach the Vee road (R668) at a hairpin bend (043 119). [The Vee Gap, about 2.5km from the Way, is the highest point on this road as it passes below the Sugarloaf, 663m, to the east and Point 630m to the west.] As you emerge onto the road you will be rewarded with fine views of the rich pastures of the Golden Vale below you to the north.

Follow the road gently downhill until just before the bridge over the Glenlough River where you turn right down a forest track beside the river. After about 0.6km turn left along a track, cross the river and a road, and soon after the road turns right along a winding track which takes you down to the road at 026 132. Walk this road to the picturesque small town of Clogheen which marks the end of the East Munster Way and the beginning of the Avondhu Way.

N.B. The East Munster Way is not marked on the current edition of Sheet 75.

Distance: 34km / 21 miles. Ascent: 910m / 3,000ft Walking time: 9–11 hours.

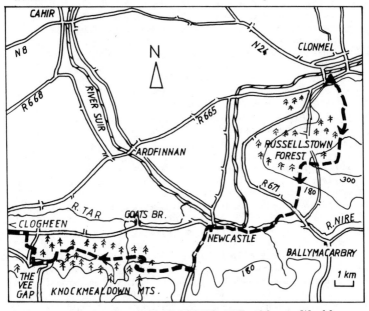

Reference: (i) OS Maps Sheets 74 & 75 (1:50,000); (ii) East Munster Way Map Guide (1:50,000), East / West mapping.

54. TEMPLE HILL–MONABRACK HORSESHOE

Driving east from Kilbeheny on the N8 take the second road on the left. After about 2km / 1.2miles you will pass a pump-house and just beyond this the road forks and you should take the right option. There is some parking at the end of the tarred section of the road, near the corner of the wood (868 197).

Here you are at an elevation of over 300m and a clear day will enable you to enjoy the splendid views in all directions — particularly scenic and including my favourite section of the Galtees with long, deep valleys from which rise the grassy-sloped peaks. The lower slopes are densely forested.

After you have lingered awhile admiring the peaks you should walk northeastwards in the direction of Monabrack — the 629m peak which is unnamed on the OS map — for 400m along a dirt track. Take the first gateway on the left and follow a contouring track to the ruins of a farmhouse. From here, it is advisable to take a sharp left turn in order to avoid a deep ravine and other obstructions and go straight down (southwest) through three small fields. This brings you to a cart track on the banks of the Behanagh River.

Proceed north along this track, cross a bridge, go through double gates and take the left-hand valley in a westerly direction. The going is easier if you keep the stream on your left. Soon, the valley swings north past the curious outcrop of Pigeon Rock on the slopes of Knocknascrow.

This is a delightful little place with its interlocking spurs, totally cutting off all views except the enclosing mountains — a perfect spot to rest and listen to the sounds of the birds and sheep who inhabit this wilderness paradise by the rushing waters of the Pigeon Rock River.

Just beyond Pigeon Rock the slope eases and you can now begin to ascend along a minor stream bed in a northwest direction. Now, views of Knockaterriff and beyond, the summit cone of Galtymore, unfold. The top of the ridge is soon reached, giving extensive valley views in all directions.

Proceeding along the ridge in a direction west of north, the great summit cairn of Temple Hill is soon reached, 785m. Descending eastwards from Temple Hill, swing slightly south to avoid the gullies running into the Glen of Aherlow. After reaching the Temple Hill–Knockaterriff col, proceed in a northeast direction to the col south of Lyracappul.

From here a short climb up a grassy slope brings you to the summit rocks of Lyracappul (Confluence of the Horse, 825m). Now follow the wall for about 1km and take a sharp turn in the direction just east of south towards Monabrack, 629m.

Time to pause again and view the evidence of turf cutting in the past, much of it for burning in the local creameries. To the northwest, there are further cuttings at 670m between Lyracappul and Knockaterriff, and a path to the area can still be discerned. Horse sleighs used to bring out the turf over the grassy terrain can still be found in local barns.

A short rise will take you to the broad summit plateau of Monabrack.

Descending from here and heading south you will soon cross a fence from where you should be able to pick out your vehicle ahead of you.

Make for the right-hand side of the small clump of trees, and from here a cart track leads you directly back to your starting point.

Distance: 14.5km/9miles. Ascent: 730m/2,400ft. Walking time: 5½ hours.

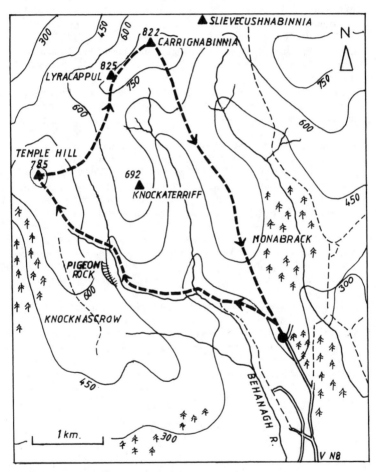

Reference OS Map: Sheet 74 (1:50,000).

55. GALTY WALL AND GALTYMORE

The starting point for this route is the same as for Walk 54. See the previous walk and follow instructions to the track on the bank of the Behanagh River.

Follow this track north along the bank of the Behanagh River. Proceed 150m beyond a wooden bridge and double gates, then follow a track and dry-stone wall northwards.

Magnificent loose stone walls are an interesting feature of this area. A similar wall runs along the top of the ridge from Lyracappul to within approx. 60m of Galtymore. These walls built about 1880 formed the boundary between the estates of the Buckleys, landlords of Galty Castle, and the Massey Estate.

Follow the wall northwards to its end and, at the ruins of what was once a substantial farmhouse on the 380m contour, continue contouring for about 0.8km where you will again pick up a track descending very gently to where it crosses a ford with a concrete base. At the western side of the ford you will be able to pick out signs of old potato ridges.

After crossing the ford, follow a path of long zigzags to where it finally peters out among turf cuttings. Continue in a northwest direction up a long spur. Eventually the slope eases and shortly afterwards you reach the wall along the top of the ridge. All your efforts are rewarded by spectacular views into the Glen of Aherlow and far beyond if the day is clear.

Follow the wall eastwards at first. Above Lake Curra it runs south-eastwards. Above the cliffs of the corrie is a perfect place to rest and absorb the splendid views in all directions. Thus refreshed, continue along the wall to where it finally runs out and there is now only a short ascent eastwards to Galtymore, 919m. Outside of Kerry, Galtymore is the highest point in Munster.

From Galtymore, the easiest way home is to retrace your steps until you are on the ridge above Lake Curra. Then follow a line east of south aiming for a few isolated deciduous trees just to the north side of Monabrack wood. This would make an excellent site for those wishing to camp.

Just below the trees you should be able to cross the stream and follow a rough track into Monabrack wood. A forest road takes you south, right through the woodland, and eventually leads to a public tarred road and back to your car.

Distance 16km/10miles. Ascent: 640m/2,100ft. Walking time: 5½ hours.

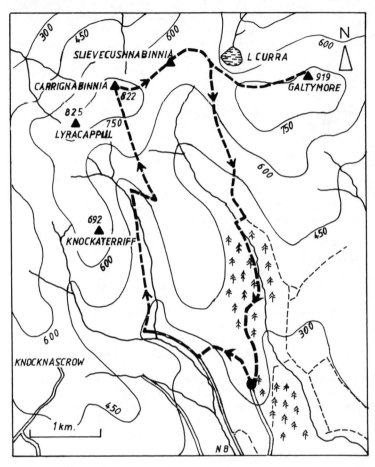

Reference OS Map: Sheet 74 (1:50,000).

56. GALTYMORE BY THE 'BLACK ROAD'

Galtymore is the highest peak in Munster outside of County Kerry and as such is the dominant feature of the landscape of north Munster. It is clearly visible from most main roads in south Tipperary but its twin-peak profile is best seen from the N8 (the main Cahir–Mitchelstown road).

The 'Black Road', an old turf track, rises to 640m just under Galtybeg and the main Galty ridge. The ease of access this gives makes the ascent of Galtymore the least demanding and one of the most popular Irish Munros. In recent years Galtymore has tended to attract large numbers of walkers, especially on Sundays, but solitude is still to be found there during the week.

The approach is from the Mitchelstown to Cahir stretch of the N8. Coming from Mitchelstown, take the minor road on the left, 0.5km/0.3mile east of Skeheenarinky limestone schoolhouse. A disused pub a few metres beyond the corner will confirm the junction for you (907 176).

Drive straight up the minor road ignoring all forks, until you reach the end of the tarred section. Here you will find a small car park on your right (893 205).

Walk through two gates, taking care to close them after you, and follow the track known as the Black Road to its end, immediately south of Galtybeg.

From here, walking in a northwestern direction and rising gently, you will soon arrive at the col between Galtybeg and Galtymore.

As this is a sheltered spot with new views northwards towards the Glen of Aherlow and beyond, you are encouraged to rest awhile and have a snack.

Thus fortified you are well prepared to tackle the only hard work of the day's outing — the summit slopes of Galtymore. At the summit, 919m, you will find a discreet cross laboriously put in position by Ted Kavanagh and friends from Tipperary Town. You may also come across a plaque put there by the late Colonel Blake, who for many years organised an annual ascent of Galtymore on Whit Sunday.

From the summit descend first to the southwest and then along a broad spur in a southeast direction, aiming for the most northerly tip of Cooper's Wood.

Here, at the confluence of two streams is a most attractive little place to rest when the sun shines. When, finally, you have to press on, do so by following a rough path which heads uphill along the eastern side of the wood. Tracks in a southeastern direction will rejoin the Black Road just above the higher gate.

Distance: 10km/6miles. Ascent: 580m/1,900ft. Walking time: 4 hours.

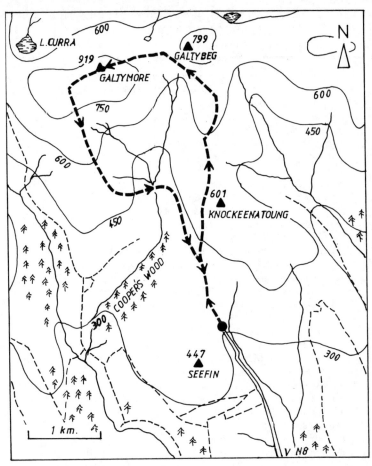

Reference OS Map: Sheet 74 (1:50,000).

57. GALTYMORE, GALTYBEG, O'LOUGHNAN'S CASTLE FROM MOUNTAIN LODGE YOUTH HOSTEL

This route is very popular among hill-walkers using Mountain Lodge Youth Hostel as a base. The hostel is situated deep in Glengara Wood 3.2km/2miles off the N8, 12.9km/8miles west of Cahir on the southern slopes of the Galtees. Occasionally in summer the wood gate maybe locked, in which case you will have more opportunities to enjoy the grandeur of this wood by walking from its edge. Glengara means Rough Glen and walkers not familiar with the wood are advised to keep to the path!

Starting from the main bridge near the youth hostel (922 209), follow the forest road uphill on the east bank of the stream. This forest road after about 2km leads to the northwest corner of Glengara Wood. Leave the road at an extremely acute right-hand bend where open ground is less than 50m away.

Cross the first stream where the bank is low, at least 100m from the corner of the wood. Continue in a westerly direction and cross another stream. Bearing northwest you should soon pick up traces of an old track going your way, eventually joining the Black Road at the col north of Knockeenatoung. Here you have joined the route to Galtymore described in Walk 56.

Follow the Black Road the short distance north to its end; then bear northwest, rising very slightly, and you will pick up a slightly worn path leading to the col between Galtybeg and Galtymore. A few hundred metres below the col on the northern side is Lake Diheen (Tub) said to be inhabited by a snake banished there by St Patrick for eternity.

From the col your route rises sharply westwards to Galtymore, 919m, frequented by Spenser who called it 'Old Father Mole'.

After a short rest, retrace your steps towards Galtybeg and if you are thirsty keep an eagle eye open for the spring on the east slope of Galtymore. Having reached the col once again prepare for the short ascent of Galtybeg, 799m. Here the ridge is at its narrowest and you can at once enjoy views on both north and south sides.

Continue eastwards to the next col and ascend the gradual slopes towards O'Loughnan's Castle, a rocky outcrop at the east end of a broad plateau. This particular spot offers excellent shelter and is a favourite place to rest and restore lost energy. A short stroll over to the edge of the cliffs will be rewarded by an excellent view of Lake Muskry. The outcrop itself is a clearly visible landmark from many of the roads to the north and southwest.

Bearing southwest will bring you to the northern edge of Glengara Wood where you are advised to enter the wood at the point of exit.

Distance : 14.5km/9miles. Ascent: 880m/2,900ft. Walking time 5½ hours.

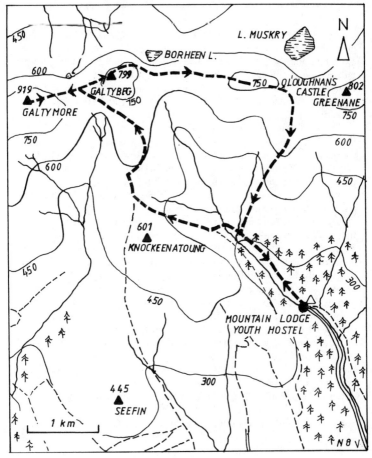

Reference OS Map: Sheet 74 (1:50,000).

58. GALTYMORE FROM THE GLENCUSH BOREEN

Even though this is a steep ascent it is the most popular and most direct route up Galtymore from the north side. It is the route followed when all and sundry climb the mountain on the organised annual climb on Whit Sunday.

All walks on the north side of the Galtees are approached from access points in the Glen of Aherlow. From Bansha, on the N24 Tipperary to Cahir road, take the road running southwest to Rossadrehid (927 292), a tiny village due north of Lake Muskry. From Mitchelstown, take the R513 towards Limerick. After 10km/6miles turn right on the R662 and after 2.4km/1.5miles turn right again for about 17.7km/11miles towards Rossadrehid.

Driving west from Rossadrehid for 5.5km/3.5miles you reach the Clydagh Bridge (874 280). There is a narrow tarred boreen running southwards on the east side of the stream. Car drivers are advised to drive only 1.2km/0.8mile up the wide section of this boreen where they will find parking at sheep pens on the right.

Walk to the end of the Glencush boreen. Follow a faint path across the moor to where it peters out after crossing a stream.

The moraine bank of Lake Diheen now confronts you and you should first head for the gully at its western end and then bear well right up the steep, grassy slopes to the summit of Galtymore, 919m. For those not accustomed to hill-walking this is a far tougher and steeper route than the route on the Black Road from the south, described in Walk 56.

Having rested and enjoyed the views from the top, most will carefully retrace their steps back to the start. If the weather is fine, some will be tempted by the less steep but slightly longer route down to Dawson's Table (which is incorrectly marked on the OS map) and over Slievecushnabinnia to follow the long, easy spur to the north until almost in line with the top edge of Drumleagh Wood and rejoin the end of the Glencush boreen.

For Galtymore direct
Distance: 8km/5miles. Ascent: 760m/2,500ft. Walking time: 4 hours.

For the route continuing around Lake Curra add half an hour to your time.

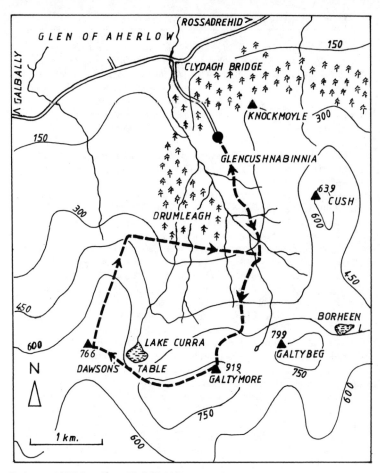

Reference OS Map: Sheet 74 (1:50,000).

59. CIRCUIT OF LAKE MUSKRY

Lake Muskry is the largest of the Galty lakes and was formerly known as Lough Bel Sead (Lake with the Jewel Mouth, the name being taken from a story in the Speckled Book of the MacEgans*). This told of the lake being the dwelling place of lovely maidens who were transformed into birds, every second year, one in particular becoming the most beautiful in the world. In keeping with her position she was allowed to wear a gold necklace which had a large jewel sparkling in it — and the name of the lake derives from this.*

Leave the N24 (Cahir–Tipperary road) at Bansha and take the road running southwest into the scenic Glen of Aherlow to the village of Rossadrehid (927 292).

Take the road running south from the village and as you enter the wood turn right along a contouring forest track. Drive about 0.7km / 0.4mile as far as a triangular section of woodland. Turn left through the barrier and go to a small, grey, brick building on the right. Park here.

Follow the main forest in a direction at first east of south and then south along the west bank of the large stream. As you leave the woods, a rising rough track gives excellent views of the Lake Muskry Cliffs topped by O'Loughnan's Castle — a rocky outcrop of glacial origin. The track levels out after a while and shortly leads you directly to Lake Muskry.

There are a number of possibilities now. If time and energy are limited, you can walk around the lake and return by the route you came.

Alternatively, climb to the top of the ridge by the steep grassy slope to the right of the cliffs, after which a short walk to the southeast will take you to O'Loughnan's Castle, the curious outcrop perched in the middle of peat hags that resembles an old building.

From here, rising gently, make your way eastwards towards Greenane (*An Grianan*, The Summer Bower, 802m), a flat summit with a triangulation pillar.

Continue in a northeast direction for 1.5km across a broad plateau until you reach what is possibly a ruined booley — Farbreaga. Booleying (farmers living in small stone shelters and grazing their cattle on the hillsides during the summer) took place here until the middle of the last century.

From here, head northwest and enter the woods at your exit point.

a) To Lake Muskry and back
Distance: 9.6km / 6miles. Ascent: 400m / 1,300ft. Walking time: 3½ hours.

b) Circuit of the Corrie
Distance: 13km / 8miles. Ascent: 760m / 2,500ft. Walking time: 5 hours.

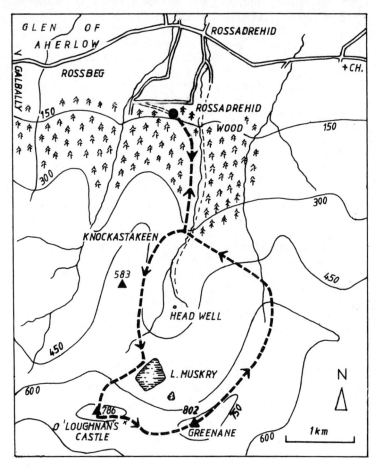

Reference OS Map: Sheet 74 (1:50,000).

60. GLENCUSH HORSESHOE

This is the most attractive and exhilarating walk in the Galtees, taking in views of all the Galty corries and lakes.

For directions to the starting point see instructions on access to the Clydagh Bridge (5.6km/3.5miles west of Rossadrehid) in Walk 58.

Drive 220m up the Glencushnabinnia boreen and park at the first wood entrance on the right. Walk up the boreen as far as the edge of the forest on your left.

From here head directly for Cush, 639m. On its southern side a deep and sometimes boggy col is encountered on your way to Galtybeg, 799m, the ice-sculptured northeast face of which is seen at its best from this angle of approach. Another shallower col follows as you head west and begin the ascent of Galtymore, keeping an eye open for the permanent spring on the way up.

On the summit itself, 919m, the tradition of having a cross has been continued. The present cross, a discreet metal one, was erected to replace a stone one damaged by storms.

Descending from Galtymore the route picks up the wall running along the ridge above Lake Curra. Leave the wall and head north along a broad spur, eventually taking the easy slopes towards the western edge of Drumleagh Wood in the distance. Aim for the middle of the forest edge. Walk northwards along the edge until you see a forest road just inside. This road leads downhill to your car.

Distance: 10km/6miles. Ascent: 1,030m/3,400ft. Walking time: 5 hours.

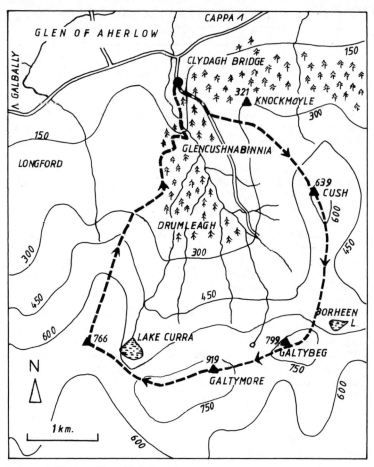

Reference OS Map: Sheet 74 (1:50,000).

61. BALLYDAVID WOOD YOUTH HOSTEL TO MOUNTAIN LODGE YOUTH HOSTEL

This walk between the two Galty youth hostels is easily accomplished by seasoned walkers and though most of it is across the least interesting part of the ridge there are fine views.

From Ballydavid Wood Youth Hostel (979 285) in the Glen of Aherlow (2.4km/1.5miles east of Rossadrehid), follow the gravel road on long zigzags to its end, then onto a steep grassy track to its end. Continue along a rough track southwest until it crosses a forest road. Follow a narrow track for 300m where you should find another track branching off to the right (westwards). Follow this to the edge of the wood.

Shortly after coming out onto the open moorland you will reach cairned Sturrakeen (Little Stump, approx. 500m).

There is no trail as such even though there are occasional stone markers so far apart that they merely reassure you that you are on route rather than keep you on it.

From Sturrakeen continue southwest across boggy ground to a rocky outcrop, 597m, and, holding the same direction, follow a slight rise to the cairn–surmounted peak which I take to be Laghtshanaquilla (Rocks of the Old Crock, 631m).

From it the route bears west and is defined now by traces of a ruined ditch which crosses numerous deep hags floored by a mixture of black peat and pink sandstone debris. Rise to what is probably a ruined booley (Farbreaga) at the eastern end of the Greenane plateau. The stone markers reappear here taking you to the flat summit of Greenane (*An Grianan*, The Summer Bower, 802m) and along this stretch you have before you a superb view of Galtymore dominated by the ridge.

From Greenane, the most direct route is a line just west of south towards the northeast corner of Glengara Wood. From this corner go west for 600m and pick up a grassy firebreak leading to a forest road where you turn left and go directly down to the hostel.

Distance: 10.9km/6.8miles. Ascent: 760m/2,500ft. Walking time: 4½ hours.

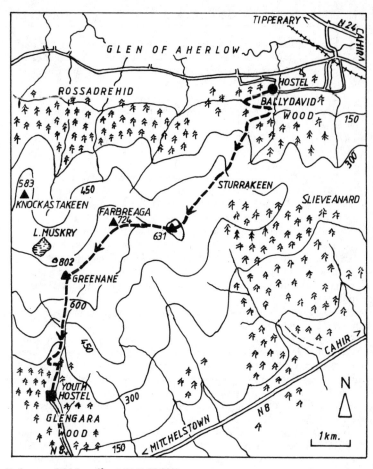

Reference OS Map: Sheet 74 (1:50,000).

62. GALTY RIDGE WALK

The traverse of the Galty Mountains is about 26km long and runs roughly east–west, ending or beginning in the historical town of Cahir. It is a superb ridge walk which includes five peaks over 800m and its highest peak, Galtymore, 919m, is one of the few Irish Munros.

It is a demanding walk and the eastern third requires very precise navigation in misty conditions. It doesn't matter which direction one takes but I prefer to start at the western end to get the ascent of Temple Hill behind me early in the day. However, that means the roughest ground and least interesting section is left until the evening.

Take the N8 north from Mitchelstown and just past Kilbeheny take the first road on your left. Drive to where the road cuts through a farmyard. Then, 100m or so further on at a sharp bend there is a wooden gate leading to a grassy track. There is parking for only one car here (857 194).

Walk up this track and along a fence towards the southern spur of Temple Hill. Along the route you may come across a relatively new rough track running in your direction. This goes to within 70m of the top.

The summit of Temple Hill, 785m, is dominated by a very large and impressive cairn, one of the many prehistoric burial grounds found on Irish peaks.

From here descend eastwards for 180m, over small boulders to a col, then northeast for 60m to another col between Knockaterriff and Lyracappul. This area requires careful navigation to avoid dropping too low below the first or second cols. In recent years this part of the Galtees has been explored in search of gold but efforts so far have yielded nothing.

The route continues upwards to Lyracappul and the little cairn at the top, 825m. A high stone wall runs from this point and it can be followed along the crest of the ridge for the next 6km to within 60m of Galtymore, passing the summit cairns of Carrignabinnia, 822m, and Slievecushnabinnia, 766m, along the way. The wall passes close to the cliffs above Lough Curra — a corrie lake on the northern slopes of the ridge. From here it is only 20 minutes to the highest point in the southeast of Ireland — Galtymore, 919m — and a superb viewpoint.

The route now descends westwards for 200m to a col above Lake Diheen. Two-thirds of the way down you will come across a permanent spring which is a very welcome sight on an otherwise 'dry' route. Then a gradual ascent towards Galtybeg, from where you again drop down to another col with Lake Borheen beneath it to the north.

The route now crosses a plateau area towards the outcrop known as O'Loughnan's Castle. This is a rather featureless and peaty section and, in mist, care should be taken to avoid dropping too low on the south side.

O'Loughnan's Castle is a rocky outcrop sculptured by frost shattering

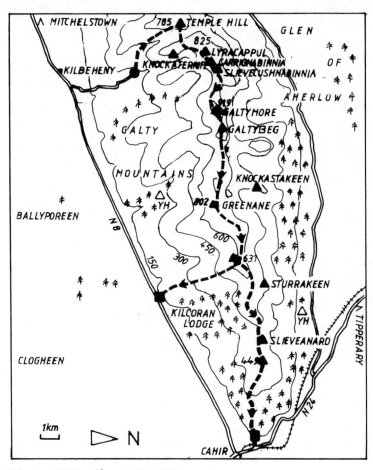

Reference OS Map: Sheet 74 (1:50,000).

during glacial times. Below it to the north is the largest and most attractive of the corrie lakes — Lake Muskry.

A short walk through peat hags and stoney ground takes you to the Greenane trig. point at 802m. Crossing the plateau in a northeast direction you will encounter occasional small cairns until you come to the end of the plateau known as Farbreaga. This can be identified by the presence of a ruined shelter and it marks an important directional change. From the col, follow a low earth-bank running east through a series of deep peat hags until you reach the cairn north of 631m. This cairn marks the change in direction to the next col and peak, 597m. This is a broad col with a small outcrop. (Walkers heading for the Ballydavid Wood Youth Hostel should go northeast along the spur towards Sturrakeen — see Walk 61.)

For those heading for Cahir, continue up to 541m. The terrain is tedious and navigation difficult in this area. The route now drops down to the col west of Slieveanard. Here the woods on the north and south are only 100m apart. Slieveanard itself is marked only by a small cairn adjoining a rough forest track.

N.B. From Slieveanard onwards much of the area shown on the OS Sheet 74 as being forested is still open moorland.

Next the direction is northeast and it is only 60m uphill to the trig. point at 449m. From here take a bearing to the corner of the woods with a small sheep pen. A narrow grassy track drops steeply downhill crossing a forest road.

Cross a gate and veer left along a track at the edge of the wood towards a bungalow on a tarred road. Continue down this road for a short distance to the 'seat at the top of the mountain road' where your car awaits you (1.5km/1mile from Cahir).

Distance: 27km/17miles. Ascent: 1,500m/4,900ft. Walking time: 8–10 hours.

At point 631m walkers may wish to head south along the spur west of Kilcoran Lodge Wood and finish on the Cahir–Mitchelstown road (N8), avoiding the rough ground and least interesting section of the ridge.

Distance: 22km/14miles. Ascent: 1,150m/3,800ft. Time: 7–8½ hours.

KEY MAP TO GALTY MOUNTAIN WALKS

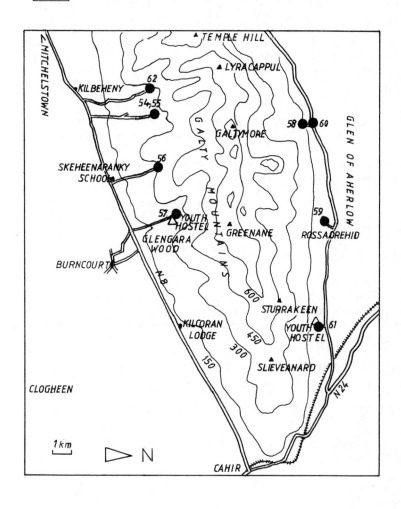

63. THE BALLYHOURA MOUNTAINS

The eastern Ballyhouras (Bealach Fheabhrat, *Pass of Feabhrat*) *comprise a relatively narrow plateau distinguished by a number of conglomerate outcrops with interesting and unusual formations.*

From the village of Ardpatrick (642 212), take the R512 (L36) south along the road to Fermoy. Turn right after 0.8km/0.5mile, at the first crossroads, and drive uphill for 1.4km/0.9mile. Park here (Toor).

Begin walking uphill along the main forest road and out onto the open moorland. Leave the road when you get to the col at 638 186. Follow a low earth-bank eastwards as far as point 516, avoiding the thick heather so characteristic of these hills. It is marked by a triangulation point and TV Booster station. Drop down slightly and follow a well-worn path southwards towards Seefin, which at 528m is the highest point of the Ballyhouras. Unlike the other high areas there is no tor here, the summit instead crowned by what is said to be the burial cairn of Finn McCool's poet son Oisin.

Return to the start by retracing your steps (or alternatively head south towards Long Mountain, visiting each of the tors in turn; but walking through the long vegetation can be very tedious).

Distance: 6.4km/4miles. Ascent: 290m/950ft. Walking time: 2¼ hours.

B. Seefin: Alternative route

Follow the R512 south from Ardpatrick for 3.2km/2miles. Take a right turn and drive along this third-class road for a further 3.2km/2miles. Park near a bird illustration board. Proceed along a grassy track which rises gently towards the summit of Seefin, 528m.

Distance: 4km/2.5miles. Ascent: 280m/910ft. Walking time: 1½ hours.

If you can arrange the necessary transport, a more interesting walk would be to start from A (Toor), walk over Seefin and descend to B, the start of the alternative route.

Distance: 5.5km/3.5miles. Ascent: 290m/950ft. Walking time: 2 hours.

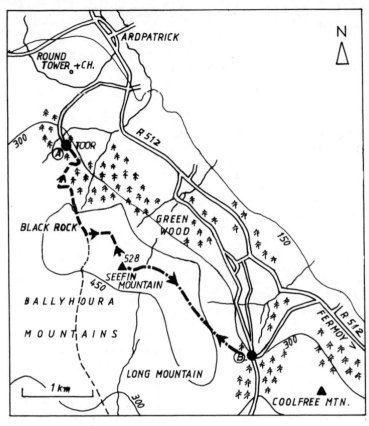

Reference OS Map: Sheet 73 (1:50,000).

64. SILVERMINES AND KEEPER HILL

This pleasant horseshoe includes crossing the River Mulkeir in two places. It is important to find the best crossing points as it is a substantial river which is too wide and too deep to ford.

Take the R499 west from Silvermines village and after about 4km/ 2.5miles you will come to a junction where you take the road running south. After 3.2km/2miles turn in to the river valley between the Silvermines ridge to the north and Keeper Hill to the south. After about 1.6km/1mile along it, park close to a farm surrounded by trees on the left (792 692).

Cross the fields by the farm and head uphill in a northeasterly direction until you reach the top of the ridge at about 390m. Then turn right and follow the edge of low crags. From here it is very easy walking on a mixture of rock and boggy terrain to the little cairn at 460m. The highest point of the ridge is reached further along, 489m.

There are fine views south across the valley to Keeper Hill. Below you on the left are the ugly waste heaps of the mines for which the mountain is named. Lead, zinc and silver were first found in this area in the fourteenth century but mining is not carried on any longer.

Soon after 489m, you drop down to a col which leads to the first of the forests which almost cover the eastern end of the ridge. A stream flows southwards by the edge of the forest. Before reaching the trees turn right and head down the southern side of the hill towards the road in the valley. Use a concealed gate about 100m from forest edge. Turn right towards a lane leading to a farm on the bank of the Mulkeir River. The lane goes through the farmyard. Just behind the farmyard, turn left towards the river where you will find a timber footbridge spanning what is otherwise a difficult stream to cross.

Now start uphill again, southwards along a dirt track and through fields towards Keeper Hill. This is a tedious ascent of over 500m through thick heather and long grassy vegetation, and you will be relieved to reach the summit cairn, 694m. The view from the summit is rewarding with the Silvermines ridge to the north and numerous low hills, often wooded, dominating the landscape in all directions. It was on the west side of Keeper Hill in 1690 that Patrick Sarsfield and his men camped before successfully ambushing the Williamite siege train at Ballyneety, Co. Limerick.

From the summit cairn, head downhill towards the northwest corner of the plateau where two small stone piles overlook a roughly circular bed of boulders probably prehistoric in origin. Just beyond them is the attractive little corrie of Eagle's Nest. The corrie itself does not contain a lake and is forested. Above the forest there are a number of crags not shown on the OS map, which could be dangerous in misty conditions.

Now make your way round the rim of the corries and then northwest towards a large forest. Drop down to the corner of the forest and a dirt track (this track is used by cattle and could be very muddy in winter). Turn left and walk along the track until you come to derelict farm buildings. Cross two fields by the farm, keeping to the left until you come to a gate leading to a green road. Follow this road to the rough track which continues down to the river; cross here by a bridge and you will then emerge close to where you parked your car.

Distance: 11.3km/7miles. Ascent: 830m/2,750ft. Walking time: 5 hours.

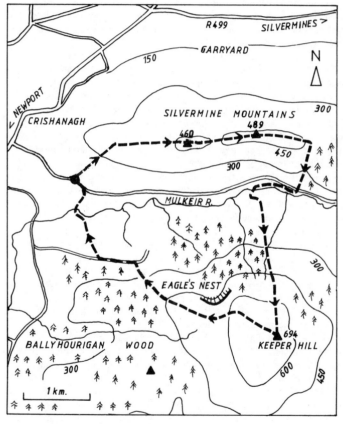

Reference OS Map: Sheet 59 (1:50,000).

65. GLENLETTER CIRCUIT

*The Slieve Bloom do not get the attention they deserve, perhaps because
they are a bit far from Dublin for a day trip and not far enough for a
weekend. But if the hilltops are not very exciting, there are some fine valley
circuits, where you will find mixed woodlands, enough open ground to command
views, and pleasant upland streams. This walk and the next one are a good
introduction.*

From Cadamstown take the R421 southwest towards Kinnitty for
2km/1.2miles. At Lackaroe Crossroads turn left (signposted Glenletter)
and continue for 5km/3miles to the car park at the forest entrance 100m
beyond Letter Crossroads (254 044).

From the car park walk south of east uphill on the tarred road for
1.5km. Take the gravel road to the left passing the triangulation point for
Wolftrap Mountain, 487m, on your right and continue on this gravel road
to its end among the forest communications masts and stay wires.

At the end of the road continue due north across the heather to the edge
of the forest plantation. The panoramic views to the north and west are
spectacular. At the edge of the forest you could find a deer track which will
greatly ease your passage through the heather northwest towards the
unmarked summit of Spink, 330m.

On your way you will pass some small turf banks still in use and others
abandoned to the encroaching heather. These turf banks are shallow, being,
as is said, only two boards deep — a board being the depth of turf sod cut
by the slean. Continue from the turf banks by the bog road which leads to
a forest road.

At the forest road (253 071) turn left, southwest. From this point you are
on the route of the Slieve Bloom Way and the markers with their yellow
arrows will be an aid to your route finding. One hundred metres further
on, cross the stile to the left of the wooden gate and continue on the forest
road through the plantation to the river valley below.

Cross the Silver River at the ford, continue up the road and turn left
(due south) at the small junction (253 074).

Approx. 1km along this rough road, at the edge of the river, enter the
forest plantation by the wooden gate on the right (236 067). This small path
was in times past a laneway to a now long abandoned cottage which you
will pass farther on.

The walk continues along a wide forest cutting which will no doubt
become a forest road in the future. Where the cutting eventually meets the
plantation road proper, turn left due west and continue to the tarred
country road above.

At this tarred road (229 057) turn due south and you will have fine views of Glenletter and Barlahan (*Barr*, summit/top; *lahan*, broad) as you make your way along this road to Letter Crossroads and the car park.

Distance 14.5km/9miles. Ascent: 300m/980ft. Walking time: 4 hours.

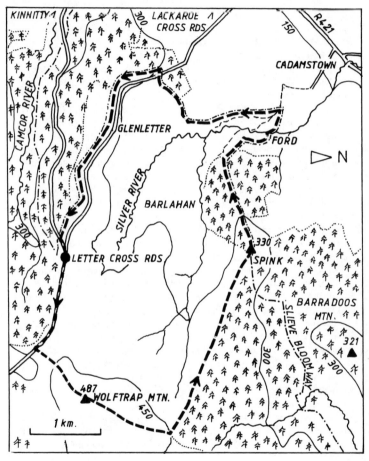

Reference OS Map: Sheet 54 (1:50,000).

66. GLENBARROW CIRCUIT

From the village of Rosenallis take the road for Mountrath and 1.3km/0.8mile from Rosenallis at a T-junction turn right (northwest).

Take note that many signposts are brown and white. These are direction signposts to amenity areas.

Follow the direction signpost indicating Glenbarrow Valley Forest Walk and 2km/1.2miles along this straight road, at a small crossroads, turn southwest into Glenbarrow.

1.5km/1mile along this winding lane you arrive at Glenbarrow car park (368 082), the start of this walk and also the start of the long-distance walk the Slieve Bloom Way.

From the car park take the lane signposted to the Ridge of Capard. Continue along the forest road and 1.5km further on, at the forest boundary, turn left southeast and continue uphill to the ridge.

Leaving the metal pylons of the telecommunications relay station behind you on your left, follow the markers of the Slieve Bloom Way, taking the rough track southwest for 50m to the tarmac road.

From the tarmac road continue southwest across the heather along the ridge, crossing a track which leads to the forest plantation visible on your right. Do not be tempted to continue on this track until nearer the plantation as the ascent to the ridge from that point is through sodden marsh and deep heather. Keep high on the ridge where the shorter heather gradually gives way to the bedrock of the mountain range.

In the distance, weather permitting, the large stone cairn known locally as the Stoney Man will be visible (347 048). This cairn is often mistaken for the summit of Clarnahinch Mountain, 483m, but is in fact a cairn on the spoil heap of a small, long-abandoned sandstone quarry. The hollows at the cairn are an excellent spot to shelter from the driving rain or chilling wind or to have lunch and appreciate the views as far northeast, east and southwest as the eye can see. In ideal conditions the mountains of Wicklow, the Blackstairs, Comeraghs, Silvermines and Galtees can be seen.

At this point you leave the Slieve Bloom Way to continue southwest from the cairn over the heather-clad unmarked summit of Clarnahinch Mountain to the col beyond.

Baunreaghcong, 509m, with its small, heathery cairn rises from the far side of the col. The easiest line of ascent is alongside the deep furrow ploughed before the upland blanket bog became a National Nature Reserve.

From Baunreaghcong continue west/northwest for almost 2km to Barna, 504m. When plodding through the energy-sapping heather, the hill-walkers' rest (to stop for the view or the photograph!) is richly rewarded

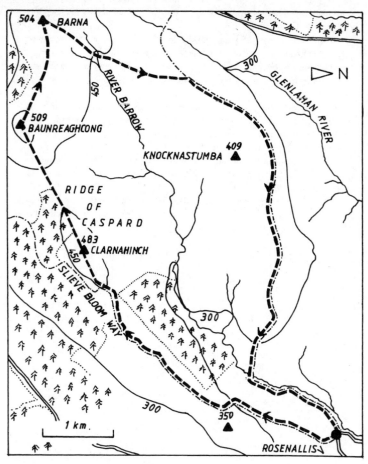

Reference OS Map: Sheet 54 (1:50,000).

with the complete panorama of Glenbarrow and views across the Bog of Allen far to the north.

From the summit of Barna, marked by a heather-covered cairn, descend north/northeast to the source of the River Barrow, and continuing in the same direction you will shortly rejoin the Slieve Bloom Way. Head first in a northeast direction and then eastwards overlooking the Glenlahan Valley on your left.

As you walk along, you will see the stumps of the ancient pine forest which covered this area some 6,000 years ago, now uprooted and exposed in the course of modern forest planting. Some stumps still cling to their leathery bark long preserved in the bog.

When the pylons on the opposite side of the valley become visible, keep a watch for the Slieve Bloom Way marker on the left of the road; its yellow arrow indicates the easiest way to descend to the river below.

Cross the river by way of the timber footbridge (360 069) and continue on the east bank of the river, past the waterfall, the cliffs of glacial till and along the forest path to the car park.

Distance: 16km/10miles. Ascent: 440m/1,450ft. Walking time: 5½ hours.

67. THE DEVIL'S BIT

The Devil's Bit is a curious notch clearly visible over a wide area. The devil is reputed to have bitten a large piece from the ridge of the Devil's Bit Mountain and finding it distasteful spat it out. It landed 30km south, in the Golden Vale at Cashel where it forms the 'Rock of Cashel'. However, it must have undergone a major metamorphosis, as the Rock of Cashel is limestone and the mountain of origin is composed of Silurian grits. Geologists believe the gorge known as the Gap was the result of breaching during glacial times.

From Templemore take the road (R501) southwest towards Borrisoleigh. Shortly after Barna Cross (3.2km/2miles approx.) turn right. At the T-junction turn right again and then left. Follow this narrow road as far as a large car park (062 732) facing the Devil's Bit.

A well-worn path through fields and woodland leads to the gorge known as the Gap, passing a grotto and a tower along the way. A large cross is visible on top of the steep-sided tor on the left. The cross, 13m high and made of concrete, was erected in 1953 and is permanently lit. A short scramble, 15m along a well-worn path leads up to the cross.

Descend by the same path to reach the Gap. This is the 'Bite'. Cross the 'Bite' along a path to where another short scramble will take you to the top of a bare plateau of grey Silurian rocks and low heather to a trig. station marking the summit at 480m. The plateau is bounded on all sides by low cliffs so care should be taken when descending. Therefore, it is prudent to follow the same line back to the Gap and retrace your steps to the road.

Distance: 4km/2.5miles. Ascent: 240m/800ft. Walking time: 1½ hours.

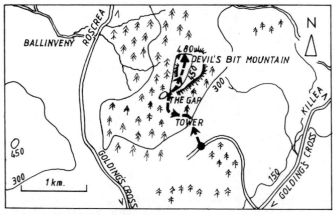

Reference OS Map: Sheet 59 (1:50,000).

BIBLIOGRAPHY

General

Charlesworth, J.K., *The Geology of Ireland — An Introduction*, London 1966.

Dillon, P., *The Mountains of Ireland*, Milnthorpe 1992.

Fairley, J., *An Irish Beast Book* (Revised ed.), Belfast 1984.

Gillmor, D. (ed.), *The Irish Countryside*, Dublin 1989.

Harbison, P., *Guide to the National and Historic Monuments of Ireland* (3rd ed.), Dublin 1992.

Harbison, P. (ed.), *The Shell Guide to Ireland*, Dublin 1989.

Herman, D., *Walking Ireland's Mountains*, Belfast 1994.

Herman, D., *Walker's Companion: Ireland*, London 1994.

Holland, C.H. (ed.), *A Geology of Ireland*, Edinburgh 1981.

Hutchinson, E.D., *Birds in Ireland*, Calton 1989.

Joyce, P.W., *Irish Names of Places* (3 vols), London 1973.

Lynam, J. (ed), *Irish Peaks*, London 1982.

Lynam, J. (ed), *Best Irish Walks*, Dublin 1998.

Mulholland, J., *Guide to Ireland's 3000-foot Mountains*, Wirral 1988.

Praeger, Robert L., *The Way that I Went*, Cork 1998.

Webb, D.A., *An Irish Flora*, Dundalk 1977.

Whittow, J.B., *Geology and Scenery in Ireland*, Harmondsworth 1974.

East

Boyle, K. & Burke, O., *The Wicklow Way — A Natural History Field Guide*, Dublin 1990.

Brunker, J.P., *The Flora of County Wicklow*, Dundalk 1950.

East West Mapping, *The Wicklow Way Map Guide* (2nd ed), Clonegal 1995.

Fewer, M., *The Wicklow Way*, Dublin 1988.

Herman, D., *Hill Walkers Wicklow*, Dublin 1992.

Herman, D., *Hill Strollers Wicklow*, Dublin 1994.

Hutchinson, C., *Birds of Dublin and Wicklow*, Dublin 1975.

Joyce, W. St J., *The Neighbourhood of Dublin*, Dublin 1971.

Lynam, J., *Walking the Blackstairs*, Borris 1994.

Malone, J.B., *The Complete Wicklow Way*, Dublin 1988.

Moriarty, C., *On Foot in Dublin and Wicklow*, Dublin 1989.

Price, L., *The Place Names of County Wicklow* (7 vols.), Dublin 1967.

Wilson, K. & Gilbert, R. (eds.), *The Big Walks*, London 1980.

Southeast and Midlands

East West Mapping, *The South Leinster Way Map Guide*, Clonegal 1995.

East West Mapping, *The East Munster Way Map Guide*, Clonegal 1995.

Joyce, T.J., *Bladhma. Walks of Discovery in Slievebloom*, Rosenallis 1995.

McGrath, D., *A Guide to the Comeragh Mountains*, Waterford 1995.

Power, P.C., *Heritage Trails in South Tipperary*, Clonmel 1987.

Warner, P., *A Visitor's Guide to the Comeragh Mountains*, Belfast 1978.

Wilson, K. & Gilbert, R. (eds.), *Classic Walks*, London 1982.

Wilson, K. & Gilbert, R. (eds.), *Wild Walks*, London 1988.

GLOSSARY

Glossary of the more common Irish words used in Place Names

Abha, abhainn (ow, owen) river
Achadh (agha, augh) field
Ail or *Faill* cliff
Alt height or side of glen
Ard height, promontory
Ath ford

Baile (bally) town, townland
Bán (bawn, baun) white
Barr top
Beag (beg) small
Bealach (ballagh) pass
Beann (ben) peak or pointed mountain
Bearna (barna) gap
Bignian little peak
Bó cow
Bóthar (boher) road
Bothairin (bohereen) small (unsurfaced) road
Breac (brack) speckled
Brí (bree, bray) hill
Buaile (booley) summer dairy pasture
Buí yellow
Bun foot of anything, river mouth

Carn pile of stones
Carraig (carrick) a rock
Cathair (caher) stone fort
Ceann (ken) head, headland
Ceathramhadh (carrow) quarter of land
Ceapach plot of tillage ground
Cill cell, church
Clár plain, board
Cloch stone
Clochóg stepping stones
Cluain (cloon) meadow
Cnoc (knock, crock) hill
Coill (kyle, kill) wood
Coire cauldron, corrie
Cor rounded hill
Corrán (carraun) sickle, serrated mountain

Cruach, cruachan steep hill (rick)
Cúm (coum) hollow, corrie

Dearg red
Doire (derry) oakgrove
Druim ridge
Dubh (duff, doo) black
Dún fort, castle

Eas (ass) waterfall
Eisc (esk) steep, rocky gully

Fionn (fin) white, clear
Fraoch (freagh) heath, heather

Gabhar (gower) goat
Gaoith (gwee) wind
Glas green
Glais streamlet
Gleann (glen) valley
Gort tilled field

Inbhear (inver) river mouth
Inis island

Lágh (law) hill
Leac flagstone
Leaca, leacan (lackan) side of a hill
Leacht huge heap of stones
Learg side of a hill
Leitir (letter) wet hillside
Liath (lea) grey
Loch (lough) lake or sea inlet
Lug, lag hollow

Machaire (maghera) plain
Mael, maol (mweel) bald, bare hill
Maigh plain
Mám, madhm (maum) pass
Más long, low hill
Mór (more) big
Muing long-grassed expanse
Mullach summit

Oilean island

Poll hole, pond

Riabhach grey
Rinn headland
Rua, ruadh red

Scairbh (scarriff) shallow ford
Scealp rocky cleft
Sceilig (skellig) rock
Sceir (sker, pl. skerry) rock, reef (Norse)
Sean old
Sescenn (seskin) marsh
Sidh (shee) fairy, fairy hill
Sliabh (slieve) mountain
Slidhe (slee) road, track
Spinc pointed pinnacle
Srón nose, noselike mountain feature
Sruth, sruthair, sruthán stream
Stuaic (stook) pointed pinnacle
Súi, suidhe (see) seat

Taobh, taebh (tave) side, hillside
Teach house
Teampall church
Tír (teer) land, territory
Tobar well
Tor tower-like rock
Torc wild boar
Tulach little hill